Research and Publication Ethics
A Comprehensive Guide to Ethical Research Practices

Sheeba P. S.

To my family and friends,
for their endless support.

Contents

Preface

Welcome to "Research and Publication Ethics - A Comprehensive Guide to Ethical Research Practices", a thorough guide crafted to navigate the intricate and crucial terrain of ethical considerations in scientific research and scholarly publication. As the scientific community grows and transforms, preserving integrity and ethical standards becomes ever more crucial. This book is designed to empower researchers, educators, and students alike with the knowledge and tools essential for upholding these principles.

This book is driven by a strong dedication to cultivating a culture characterized by honesty, transparency, and accountability in both research and publication practices. Ethical lapses can profoundly impact not just individual researchers but also the wider scientific community and society as a whole. By comprehending and adhering to ethical standards, we uphold the credibility and trustworthiness of scientific knowledge.

Research and Publication Ethics is organized to offer a comprehensive examination of essential topics, challenges, and best practices in the field.

Each chapter thoroughly explores crucial facets of research and publication ethics, such as data integrity, authorship, peer review, conflicts of interest, and responsible research practices.

The book comprises of 12 chapters, starting with foundational concepts like philosophy and moral judgment, and progressing through various topics in scientific and publication ethics. It also includes a chapter dedicated to Artificial Intelligence in Research, reflecting contemporary research trends. Each chapter concludes with a summary to consolidate key points.

This book is the culmination of years of learning, not only from books and experiences but from the invaluable lessons imparted by my parents. I am deeply indebted to my family members, my husband Swayajith and son Adarsh whose constant support and encouragement throughout the writing of this textbook has been invaluable. Your love and faith in me made this accomplishment achievable.

This work has benefited greatly from contributions from diverse sources. I am thankful to my colleagues whose insights and feedback have enriched the content, and to the students whose questions and curiosity have motivated to explore these topics in greater depth. A special acknowledgment goes to our editorial team for their diligent efforts and commitment to upholding the highest standards of quality.

I trust this book will prove invaluable to all participants in the research and publication process, whether you are a new researcher, seasoned academic, or institutional leader. My aim is to assist you in achieving ethical excellence and fostering a credible and resilient scientific community.

I welcome your feedback and suggestions to enhance and update this work in future editions.

Thank you for selecting Research and Publication Ethics - A Comprehensive Guide to Ethical Research Practices. Wishing you success and integrity in all your research endeavors.

Sincerely,

Sheeba P. S.
12th September 2024.

Chapter 1

Philosophy and Ethics

1.1 What is Philosophy?

Philosophy is the systematized study of general and fundamental questions, such as those concerning existence, reason, knowledge, values, mind, and language. Philosophy in Greek means 'love of wisdom'. Some sources claim that the term was coined by Pythagoras although this theory is disputed by some. Philosophical methods include questioning, critical discussion, rational argument, and systematic presentation. Historically, philosophy encompassed all bodies of knowledge and a practitioner was known as a philosopher.

In the 19th century, the growth of modern research universities led academic philosophy and other disciplines to professionalize and specialize. Since then, various areas of investigation that were traditionally part of philosophy have become separate academic disciplines, and namely the social sciences such as psychology, sociology, linguistics, and economics. Many definitions of philosophy emphasize its intimate relation to science. In this sense, philosophy is sometimes understood as a proper science in its own right.

1.1.1 Research Philosophy

Research philosophy occupies a significant place in the field of science and education. Research philosophy is classified as ontology, epistemology and axiology. Ontology is based on the nature of reality. It is classified on the basis of objectivism and subjectivism. Epistemology is a branch of research philosophy that is aimed at studying the essence of knowledge and scientific facts. Axiology is a branch of philosophy which is concerned with judgments, aesthetics, and ethics. These philosophical approaches enable them to decide which approach should be adopted by the researcher and why, which is derived from research questions (Saunders, Lewis, and Thornhill, 2009). The important assumptions are present in research philosophy which explains the researcher's view regarding the world. These assumptions will determine the research strategy and the methods of that strategy.

A research philosophy is a framework that guides how research should be conducted based on ideas about reality and the nature of knowledge (Collis and Hussey, 2014, p.43). The two main research philosophies are positivism and interpretivism. These philosophies represent two fundamentally different ways that we as humans make sense of the world around us: in positivism, reality is independent of us and researchers can therefore observe reality objectively. In interpretivism, reality is seen as highly subjective because it is shaped by our perceptions (Collis and Hussey, 2014, p.45). Positivism originated in the natural sciences and focuses on scientific testing of hypothesis and finding logical or mathematical proof that derives from statistical analysis (Collis and Hussey, 2014, p.44. Positivists therefore tend to use large sample sizes and to produce precise, objective and quantitative data (Collis and Hussey, 2014, p.50).

1.2 What is Ethics?

Ethics, also called moral philosophy, the discipline concerned with what is morally good and bad and morally right and wrong. The term is also applied to any system or theory of moral values or principles. Ethics subject consists of the fundamental issues of practical decision making, and its major concerns include the nature of ultimate value and the standards by which human actions can be judged right or wrong.

The terms ethics and morality are closely related. It is now common to refer to ethical judgments or to ethical principles where it once would have been more accurate to speak of moral judgments or moral principles. These applications are an extension of the meaning of ethics. In earlier usage, the term referred not to morality itself but to the field of study, or branch of inquiry, that has morality as its subject matter. In this sense, ethics is equivalent to moral philosophy.

Although ethics has always been viewed as a branch of philosophy, its all-embracing practical nature links it with many other areas of study, including anthropology, biology, economics, history, politics, sociology, and theology. Yet, ethics remains distinct from such disciplines because it is not a matter of factual knowledge in the way that the sciences and other branches of inquiry are. Rather, it has to do with determining the nature of normative theories and applying these sets of principles to practical moral problems.

Traditionally, ethics referred to the philosophical study of morality, the latter being a more or less systematic set of beliefs, usually held in common by a group, about how people should live. Ethics also referred to particular philosophical theories of morality. Later the term was applied to particular (and narrower) moral codes or value systems. Ethics and morality are now used almost interchangeably in many contexts, but the name of the philosophical study remains ethics.

1.3 Moral Judgement

Moral judgment refers to a decision about what one should do in a morally problematic situation, what is right and what is wrong when deciding what to do. The cognitive-developmental approach long dominated the research domain, and moral judgment is often assessed in terms of Lawrence Kohlberg's (1984) theory of the development of moral judgments. From the 1920s to the 1950s, behaviorism was the dominant paradigm in psychology, and it was assumed that teaching children moral virtues and social norms of their culture makes them moral. It was not until Kohlberg first published results from his follow-up study of the development of moral judgments that it was more widely acknowledged that even children have their own morality and they make moral judgments that are not internalized from parents, teachers, or peers. Consequently, Kohlberg stated that morality is constructed by the person her/himself. He elaborated a stage model representing the developmental path of individuals' reasoning from preconventional to postconventional thinking. According to Kohlberg's theory, moral judgment develops through six (in empirical reality five) qualitatively different stages, which form three levels of moral reasoning: preconventional level (Stages 1 and 2); conventional level (Stages 3 and 4); and postconventional or principal level (Stage 5), and the levels are shown to be related to age and educational trends (e.g., Rest, 1994).

The moral judgments of actions (or inaction) are usually the primary focus of any discussion of Moral Judgments in particular, and Ethical analysis in general. This is because the judgments of intentions, character traits, and persons are generally based on the judgment of actions that the intention, motive, character trait, or person might potentially do or not do. So limiting the discussion to the moral judgments of actions (or inactions) will also, with suitable obvious modifications, address the moral judgment of intentions, motives, character traits and people.

1.4 Object of Moral Judgment

A moral judgement as distinguished from a factual judgement is a judgement upon the action of an individual that can be evaluated as good or bad, right or wrong. Obviously it is a judgement upon the voluntary action of the individual. Voluntary actions and habitual actions are objects of moral judgement. Non-voluntary actions are excluded from the scope of moral judgements. Habitual actions are objects of moral judgements, because they are the results repeated voluntary actions. Thus ultimately only voluntary actions are judged to be right or wrong. Whatever has not willed has no moral worth.

1.4.1 Actions

Do we judge an act by its motives or consequences? Moral judgements are not passed upon all kinds of action, but only upon conduct. But conduct or willed action has two aspects. It is will and it is action, it involves an internal factor and external factor. There is a lot of controversy between hedonists and intuitionists. Hedonists regard consequences as the object of moral judgement. Intuitionists regard motive as the object of it. The view is wrong. The idea as the end is the real motive. It induces the self to act. It is the end of action. Now, the question is to the motive or consequence of a voluntary action is the object of moral judgement which of them determines its moral quality. When there is a harmony between the inner motive and the outer consequence as a foreseen and desired.

1.4.2 Intentions

Thus we come to the conclusion that intention is the object of moral Judgement. It includes the motive or the idea of the end as well as the idea of the means. An action is good if its intention is good, in other words, if the end as well as the means adopted is good. The end never justifies the means. Thus the motive alone does not determine the moral quality of an action. Intention is the object of moral judgement. It is intention including motive that determines the moral quality of an action. An action is right when the intention of the agent is good. An action is bad or wrong if either the motive or the end and the means is bad. We may distinguish between the outer and the inner intention of an action. If a beggar comes to you; you help him in order to remove the painful feeling from your mind, which is excited by the sight of his distress, your outer intention is to help the man in distress, but your inner intention is to remove your painful feeling. The inner intention of an action is an object of moral judgement. An intention is the end that is definitely adopted as an object of will together with the means, which are consented to by the agent as necessary for the realization of the end. The intention as a whole, rather than the motive or the idea of the end is the object of moral judgement.

1.4.3 Situations

The possibility to make judgements as to how one ought to act in concrete situations requires antecedent moral principles. In the absence of such principles there is no rational basis for making such judgements. The possibility to make judgements as to how one ought to act in concrete situations implies: (1) that the situations about which we make such judgements must already have moral significance independently of the principles one may bring to bear upon them; and (2) that the rightness or wrongness of one's actions in concrete situations depends on this moral significance of situations.

1.5 Is Intention or Character the Object of Moral Judgement?

Intention is not an isolated mental phenomenon. Intention is the expression of the character. We pass moral judgements on the character of a person when we want to determine his moral worth. But we do not determine the moral quality of an action by considering the character of the agent, because a person of good character has not always a good intention and similarly a person of bad character may not have necessarily a bad intention always. So it is better to hold that intention is the object of moral judgement. Intention of the agent determines the moral quality of an action. It is wrong to hold that character is the object of moral judgement. It determines the moral worth of a person, but not of his particular actions. The moral quality of an action is always determined by the intention of the agent. The ideal or rational self is the subject of moral judgement. The spectator or the judge in a person is the ideal self.

1.5.1 Nature of Moral Judgments and Reactions

The nature of moral judgments and reactions is a complex area of study that spans several disciplines, including philosophy, psychology, neuroscience, and sociology. Overview of some key aspects and perspectives are:

1. Philosophical Perspectives

    Deontological Ethics: This approach, associated with philosophers like Immanuel Kant, asserts that moral judgments are based on rules or duties. Actions are right or wrong in themselves, regardless of the consequences.

    Consequentialism: This perspective, including utilitarianism, judges the morality of an action based on its outcomes. An action is considered right if it leads to the greatest good for the greatest number.

Virtue Ethics: Rooted in Aristotelian thought, this approach focuses on the character of the individual making the judgment. Moral actions stem from virtuous character traits like honesty, courage, and compassion.

2. Psychological Perspectives

Moral Development: Theories like Lawrence Kohlberg's stages of moral development propose that people progress through different levels of moral reasoning, from basic, self-interested reasoning to more advanced, principled reasoning.

Moral Emotions: Emotions such as guilt, shame, empathy, and indignation play crucial roles in moral judgments. Psychologist Jonathan Haidt's social intuitionist model suggests that moral judgments often arise from intuitive, emotional responses rather than deliberate reasoning.

3. Neuroscientific Perspectives

Brain Regions: Research using neuro-imaging techniques has identified brain regions involved in moral judgment, such as the prefrontal cortex, which is associated with reasoning and decision-making, and the amygdala, which is linked to emotional responses.

Moral Dilemmas: Studies often use moral dilemmas, like the famous trolley problem, to investigate how people make moral decisions and what neural processes are involved.

4. Sociological Perspectives

Cultural Relativism: This viewpoint emphasizes that moral judgments are influenced by cultural norms and practices. What is considered moral in one culture may not be in another.

Socialization: Individuals learn moral values and norms through socialization processes within their families, communities, and societies.

5. Evolutionary Perspectives

Adaptive Functions: Some theories suggest that moral behaviors and judgments have evolved because they promote social cooperation and cohesion, which are advantageous for survival and reproduction.

6. Moral Realism vs. Moral Anti-Realism

Moral Realism: The belief that there are objective moral facts and values that are independent of human beliefs and feelings.

Moral Anti-Realism: The belief that moral values are not objective and that they are constructed by humans.

7. Moral Reactions

Automatic vs. Deliberative Reactions: Moral reactions can be immediate and automatic, driven by emotions and intuitions, or they can be deliberative, involving conscious reasoning and reflection.

Contextual Influences: Factors such as situational context, social influences, and personal experiences can significantly affect moral reactions.

The study of philosophy and ethics is essential for several reasons:

i. *Intellectual Foundation:* Philosophy provides a structured framework for critically examining beliefs and assumptions. It encourages rigorous questioning and logical reasoning, fostering intellectual growth and a deeper understanding of diverse perspectives.

ii. *Moral Compass:* Ethics equips individuals with the tools to evaluate actions and their consequences, promoting moral development and responsible behavior. It helps us reflect on the impact of our decisions on others and the broader community.

iii. *Social Cohesion:* Ethical principles are vital for maintaining social order and justice. They underpin laws, policies, and social norms, ensuring fairness and protecting individual rights.

iv. *Personal Development:* Engaging with philosophical and ethical questions enhances self-awareness and personal integrity. It encourages individuals to live authentically and align their actions with their values.

v. *Global Challenges:* In an increasingly interconnected world, philosophy and ethics offer valuable insights into addressing global issues such as inequality, environmental sustainability, and technological advancements. They provide a foundation for collaborative efforts towards a just and equitable future.

By embracing the principles of philosophy and ethics, we commit to a lifelong journey of learning, reflection, and growth. This journey is essential for cultivating a more thoughtful, compassionate, and just world. Upholding these values honors our shared humanity and paves the way for a brighter future.

Ultimately, philosophy and ethics remind us that our actions matter and that each of us has a role in shaping the moral landscape of our world. Let us carry forward the lessons learned, continue to question and seek truth, and strive to live with integrity and purpose.

In summary, Philosophy and ethics form the foundation of human thought and society, guiding our understanding of the world and our place in it. Through philosophy, we explore fundamental questions about existence, knowledge, values, reason, mind, and language. Ethics, a branch of philosophy, focuses on the principles that govern our behavior, helping us distinguish right from wrong and navigate moral complexities.

Chapter 2

Scientific Conduct

Scientific conduct entails the ethical and responsible behavior required of researchers throughout all stages of the research process, from initial conception to final publication. It involves following principles such as honesty, integrity, transparency, and accountability to ensure accurate data collection and reporting, disclosure of conflicts of interest, and proper credit to all contributors. Exemplary scientific conduct also includes a commitment to rigorous peer review, ethical treatment of research subjects, and responsible dissemination of findings. Adhering to these standards is crucial for advancing knowledge, maintaining public trust, and fostering a credible and collaborative scientific community.

2.1 Ethics With Respect to Science and Research

Ethics are a set of moral principles and values a civilized society follows. Scientific pursuit is built on trust. Scientists trust that the results reported by their predecessors and peers are based on sound protocols and the conclusions drawn are valid in the light of current knowledge. Above all, the society and the tax-payer trust that the results and the projected outcome is based on an honest and conscientious attempt by the scientific community to describe the nature and phenomena accurately, without bias, and any hyperbole. A justified difference of opinion has been a part and parcel of scientific activity over the centuries.

Many different disciplines, institutions, and professions have standards for behavior that suit their particular aims and goals. These standards also help members of the discipline to coordinate their actions or activities and to establish the public's trust of the discipline. For instance, ethical standards govern conduct in medicine, law, engineering, and business. Ethical norms also serve the aims or goals of research and apply to people who conduct scientific research or other scholarly or creative activities. There is even a specialized discipline, research ethics, which studies these norms.

There are several reasons why it is important to adhere to ethical norms in research:

First, norms promote the aims of research, such as knowledge, truth, and avoidance of error. For example, prohibitions against fabricating, falsifying, or misrepresenting research data promote the truth and minimize error.

Second, since research often involves a great deal of cooperation and coordination among many different people in different disciplines and institutions, ethical standards promote the values that are essential to collaborative work, such as trust, accountability, mutual respect, and fairness. For example, many ethical norms in research, such as guidelines for authorship, copyright and patenting policies, data sharing policies, and confidentiality rules in peer review, are designed to protect intellectual property interests while encouraging collaboration. Most researchers want to receive credit for their contributions and do not want to have their ideas stolen or disclosed prematurely.

Third, many of the ethical norms help to ensure that researchers can be held accountable to the public. For instance, federal policies on research misconduct, conflicts of interest, the human subjects protections, and animal care and use are necessary in order to make sure that researchers who are funded by public money can be held accountable to the public.

Fourth, ethical norms in research also help to build public support for research. People are more likely to fund a research project if they can trust the quality and integrity of research.

Finally, many of the norms of research promote a variety of other important moral and social values, such as social responsibility, human rights, animal welfare, compliance with the law, and public health and safety. Ethical lapses in research can significantly harm human and animal subjects, students, and the public. For example, a researcher who fabricates data in a clinical trial may harm or even kill patients, and a researcher who fails to abide by regulations and guidelines relating to radiation or biological safety may jeopardize his health and safety or the health and safety of staff and students.

2.2 Codes and Policies for Research Ethics

Given the importance of ethics for the conduct of research, it should come as no surprise that many different professional associations, government agencies, and universities have adopted specific codes, rules, and policies relating to research ethics. Many government agencies have ethics rules for funded researchers.

2.2.1 Ethical Principles

The various codes addresses some of the following ethical principles:

Honesty

Strive for honesty in all scientific communications. Honestly report data, results, methods and procedures, and publication status. Do not fabricate, falsify, or misrepresent data. Do not deceive colleagues, research sponsors, or the public.

Objectivity

Strive to avoid bias in experimental design, data analysis, data interpretation, peer review, personnel decisions, grant writing, expert testimony, and other aspects of research where objectivity is expected or required. Avoid or minimize bias or self-deception. Disclose personal or financial interests that may affect research.

Integrity

Keep your promises and agreements; act with sincerity; strive for consistency of thought and action.

Carefulness

Avoid careless errors and negligence; carefully and critically examine your own work and the work of your peers. Keep good records of research activities, such as data collection, research design, and correspondence with agencies or journals.

Openness

Share data, results, ideas, tools, resources. Be open to criticism and new ideas.

Transparency

Disclose methods, materials, assumptions, analyses, and other information needed to evaluate your research.

Accountability

Take responsibility for your part in research and be prepared to give an account (i.e. an explanation or justification) of what you did on a research project and why.

Intellectual Property

Honor patents, copyrights, and other forms of intellectual property. Do not use unpublished data, methods, or results without permission. Give proper acknowledgment or credit for all contributions to research. Never plagiarize.

Confidentiality

Protect confidential communications, such as papers or grants submitted for publication, personnel records, trade or military secrets, and patient records.

Responsible Publication

Publish in order to advance research and scholarship, not to advance just your own career. Avoid wasteful and duplicate publication.

> *Responsible Mentoring:* Help to educate, mentor, and advise students. Promote their welfare and allow them to make their own decisions.

> *Respect for Colleagues:* Respect your colleagues and treat them fairly.

Social Responsibility: Strive to promote social good and prevent or mitigate social harms through research, public education, and advocacy.

Non-Discrimination: Avoid discrimination against colleagues or students on the basis of sex, race, ethnicity, or other factors not related to scientific competence and integrity.

Competence: Maintain and improve your own professional competence and expertise through lifelong education and learning; take steps to promote competence in science as a whole.

Legality: Know and obey relevant laws and institutional and governmental policies.

Animal Care: Show proper respect and care for animals when using them in research. Do not conduct unnecessary or poorly designed animal experiments.

Human Subjects Protection: When conducting research on human subjects, minimize harms and risks and maximize benefits; respect human dignity, privacy, and autonomy; take special precautions with vulnerable populations; and strive to distribute the benefits and burdens of research fairly.

2.3 Intellectual Honesty and Research Integrity

2.3.1 Intellectual Honesty

Intellectual honesty refers to the commitment to truthfulness and the avoidance of deception in the conduct, reporting, and presentation of research and scholarly work. It encompasses a range of ethical practices that ensure the accuracy and reliability of the academic record. Here are key aspects of intellectual honesty:

Accurate Reporting: Researchers must report their findings truthfully, without fabrication, falsification, or selective reporting. Data should be presented as observed, without manipulation to fit a desired outcome.

Proper Attribution: Researchers must give appropriate credit to the work and ideas of others, ensuring that all sources are properly cited. Plagiarism, or presenting someone else's work as one's own, is a severe breach of intellectual honesty.

Transparency: Researchers should be transparent about their methodologies, allowing others to replicate and verify their findings. This includes disclosing any limitations or potential biases in the study.

Acknowledging Contributions: All contributors to a research project should be properly acknowledged, and their specific contributions should be clearly defined. This includes co-authors, funders, and supporting institutions.

Avoiding Conflicts of Interest: Researchers must disclose any potential conflicts of interest that could influence their work. This includes financial, personal, or professional interests that may affect the research outcomes.

2.3.2 Research Integrity

Research integrity is the adherence to ethical principles and professional standards essential for the responsible conduct of research. It ensures that research is conducted in a fair, ethical, and professional manner. Key components of research integrity include:

Adherence to Ethical Guidelines: Researchers must follow established ethical guidelines and standards in their field, including obtaining necessary approvals for studies involving human or animal subjects.

Data Management: Researchers should maintain accurate and detailed records of their research activities, including data collection, analysis, and storage. Proper data management practices ensure the reproducibility and verification of research findings.

Peer Review: Participating in the peer review process as a reviewer and accepting feedback from peers as an author are essential for maintaining the quality and credibility of scholarly work.

Publication Ethics: Researchers must adhere to ethical standards in publishing, including avoiding duplicate publication, ensuring proper authorship attribution, and promptly correcting errors in published work.

Mentor-ship and Supervision: Senior researchers and mentors have a responsibility to guide and train junior researchers and students in ethical research practices, fostering a culture of integrity within the academic community.

Institutional Responsibility: Research institutions and organizations play a crucial role in promoting research integrity by providing training, resources, and support for ethical research practices. They should also have mechanisms in place for investigating and addressing allegations of misconduct.

2.4 Scientific Misconduct

Scientific misconduct refers to unethical behavior or practices in the conduct of scientific research. It encompasses actions that violate the fundamental principles of research integrity and intellectual honesty. Scientific misconduct can have serious consequences, including damage to the credibility of scientific research, harm to individuals or communities, and the erosion of public trust in science. The primary forms of scientific misconduct include:

Fabrication:

Fabrication involves making up data or results and recording or reporting them as if they were real.

Example: Creating fictitious experimental data or surveys that were never conducted.

Falsification:

Falsification entails manipulating research materials, equipment, processes, or changing data and results in a way that does not accurately reflect the true findings.

Example: Altering data points in a data-set to achieve desired outcomes or selectively reporting results that support a hypothesis while ignoring data that contradicts it.

Plagiarism:

Plagiarism is the appropriation of another person's ideas, processes, results, or words without giving appropriate credit.

Example: Copying text from another researcher's publication without proper citation or presenting someone else's research ideas as one's own.

Misleading Authorship:

This involves inaccurately representing the contributions of researchers in a publication, such as granting authorship to individuals who did not contribute significantly or omitting deserving contributors.

Example: Including someone as an author who did not contribute to the research or failing to include someone who did substantial work.

Duplicate Publication:

Duplicate publication, or self-plagiarism, is the practice of publishing the same material in multiple journals without acknowledgment.

Example: Submitting the same research findings to two different journals without notifying the editors.

Salami Slicing:

Salami slicing refers to the practice of dividing one significant piece of research into several smaller pieces to increase the number of publications.

Example: Publishing multiple papers with minor differences based on the same dataset to artificially inflate publication count.

Failure to Comply with Ethical Guidelines:

This involves not adhering to the ethical standards and guidelines established for conducting research, particularly those involving human or animal subjects.

Example: Conducting research on human subjects without informed consent or appropriate ethical review.

Improper Use of Funds:

Misuse of research funding for purposes not related to the approved research project.

Example: Using grant money for personal expenses or for projects not related to the grant's original purpose.

2.4.1   Consequences of Scientific Misconduct

Scientific misconduct can have far-reaching consequences, including:

Retraction of Published Work: Misconduct can lead to the retraction of published papers, which can tarnish the reputation of the researchers involved and the institutions they represent.

Loss of Funding: Researchers found guilty of misconduct may lose current and future research funding.

Damage to Reputation: Individual researchers and their affiliated institutions can suffer significant damage to their reputations.

Legal Repercussions: In some cases, scientific misconduct can lead to legal consequences, including fines and criminal charges.

Erosion of Public Trust: Scientific misconduct can undermine public trust in scientific research and its findings, which can have broader societal implications.

2.4.2 Preventing Scientific Misconduct

Preventing scientific misconduct involves fostering a culture of integrity and accountability within the research community. Key measures include:

Education and Training: Providing comprehensive training on research ethics and the responsible conduct of research to all members of the research community.

Clear Policies and Guidelines: Establishing and enforcing clear policies and guidelines on research integrity and ethical conduct.

Ethical Oversight: Implementing robust ethical review processes and oversight mechanisms to ensure compliance with ethical standards.

Promoting Transparency: Encouraging transparency in research processes, including data sharing and open communication about research practices and findings.

Addressing Conflicts of Interest: Ensuring that conflicts of interest are disclosed and managed appropriately.

Encouraging Reporting of Misconduct: Creating a safe environment for reporting suspected misconduct without fear of retaliation and ensuring that allegations are investigated thoroughly and fairly.

Accountability and Consequences: Holding individuals accountable for misconduct and ensuring that appropriate consequences are applied to deter future violations.

2.5 Redundant Publication

Redundant publication refers to the practice of publishing the same or substantially similar research findings in more than one journal or conference without proper acknowledgment or justification. This practice, also known as duplicate publication or self-plagiarism, can mislead the scientific community, waste resources, and distort the academic record.

2.5.1 Forms of Redundant Publication

Duplicate Publication:

Exact Duplicate: This occurs when the same manuscript is submitted to multiple journals simultaneously or when an author publishes the same study in more than one journal without any significant changes.

Overlapping Publication:

This involves republishing work with slight modifications, such as minor changes in the abstract, introduction, or data presentation, but essentially reporting the same research findings.

Salami Slicing (Segmented Publication):

This refers to dividing one research study into multiple smaller papers, each focusing on different aspects of the same dataset. While each "slice" may contain unique elements, the overall findings are derived from the same research project. This practice can lead to multiple publications that do not significantly contribute to the field individually.

2.5.2 Consequences of Redundant Publication

Misleading Academic Record: Authors may inflate their publication record artificially, misleading hiring committees, grant review panels, and promotion boards.

Resource Waste: Peer reviewers and editors spend valuable time and effort evaluating manuscripts, and redundant publications waste these resources.

Distortion of Scientific Literature: Redundant publications can skew meta-analyzes and systematic reviews, as the same data might be counted multiple times, leading to biased conclusions.

Damage to Credibility: Repeated instances of redundant publication can harm an author's reputation and credibility within the scientific community.

Potential Retraction: If discovered, redundant publications can lead to the retraction of the articles, damaging the author's career and the trustworthiness of the journals involved.

2.6 Selective Reporting and Misrepresentation of Data

Selective reporting and misrepresentation of data refer to practices where researchers intentionally or unintentionally present data in a misleading way. This can include omitting unfavorable results, cherry-picking data that supports a desired outcome, or altering data to fit a hypothesis. Such practices undermine the integrity of scientific research and can lead to false conclusions. It is important to use reliable sources and to critically evaluate the information presented to ensure that it is accurate and unbiased.

2.6.1 Selective Reporting

Selective reporting refers to the act of intentionally presenting or omitting certain information, data or results in a biased manner to support a particular view hypothesis or conclusion.

This can be done by presenting only the information that supports a particular argument by ignoring information that contradicts it.

Selective reporting is one type of bias which undermines the integrity of academic research. It is a large contributor to the current 'reproducibility crisis' facing scientific publishing.

Types of Selective Reporting

Publication bias: This happens when studies with significant or positive results are more likely to be published than those with non-significant or negative results. This can lead to an overestimation of the true effect size and distort the scientific literature.

Outcome reporting bias: This occurs when only certain outcomes of a study are reported, while others are omitted. Often, the reported outcomes are more favorable to the author's hypothesis or agenda.

Data dredging: This involves performing multiple statistical tests on a data-set to find significant results, even if these results are not meaningful or relevant. This practice can lead to false-positive results and is a form of data manipulation.

Spin: This happens when the presentation of results is biased or slanted towards a certain interpretation or conclusion, even if the data do not fully support it. It can be a deliberate attempt to manipulate the reader's perception of the results. Spin has been defined as a specific intentional or unintentional reporting that fails to faithfully reflect the nature and range of findings and that could affect the impression the results produce in readers.

Selective citation: This occurs when only certain studies or sources are cited to support a particular argument, while other relevant studies or sources are ignored. This is a form of cherry-picking data to support a particular viewpoint.

2.6.2 Misrepresentation of Data

It refers to the manipulation or distortion of data to create a false or misleading impression.

This can be done by selectively choosing data, altering or omitting data points, or presenting data in a way that obscures the true meaning or significance of the information.

Types of Misrepresentation of Data

Data Falsification: This occurs when data is deliberately altered or fabricated to support a particular hypothesis or conclusion. This is a grave ethical violation with severe consequences for both the individual and the organization involved. Falsification can include the manipulation of research instrumentation, materials, or processes. Manipulation of images or representations in a manner that distorts the data or "reads too much between the lines" can also be considered falsification.

Data Cherry-Picking: This involves selecting or highlighting only certain data points to support a specific conclusion, while ignoring or downplaying other data points. This practice can lead to a biased or incomplete representation of the overall data.

Data Manipulation: This occurs when data is adjusted or manipulated in a way that changes the conclusions that can be drawn from it. Examples include changing the scale of a graph's axis to exaggerate or minimize differences.

Data Misinterpretation: This happens when data is presented in a misleading way or misinterpreted. It is communicating honestly reported data in a deceptive manner. For example, one might use a statistical technique such as multiple regression or the analysis of variance to make one's results appear more significant or convincing than they really are. Or one might eliminate or trom outliers when cleaning up raw data. Examples include presenting correlation as causation or failing to consider alternative explanations for the data.

Data Omission: This occurs when relevant data is excluded from a report or analysis, either intentionally or unintentionally. This can result in an incomplete or inaccurate portrayal of the overall data.

2.6.3 How to Avoid Selective Reporting and Misrepresentation of Data

Honesty, objectivity, integrity and avoiding bias in experimental design, analysis, data interpretation, and reporting data, reults, methods and procedures in all scientific communications are optimal for research.

Ensure transparency: Be open and honest about the data being presented, including any limitations or weaknesses. This helps to avoid any perception of bias or manipulation.

Avoid cherry-picking: Present all relevant data, even if it does not support the hypothesis or conclusion being tested. This ensures that the overall picture is not skewed.

Use appropriate statistical methods: Employ suitable statistical methods to analyze the data and present the results in a way that accurately reflects the data.

Verify data sources: Confirm that the data sources are reliable and accurate to avoid errors or biases in the data.

Use independent review: Have the data and analysis reviewed by independent experts to ensure that the conclusions are sound and unbiased.

Follow ethical standards: Adhere to ethical standards and guidelines for data reporting and analysis, as established by professional organizations and regulatory bodies.

Acknowledge limitations: Be transparent about the study or analysis limitations and acknowledge any potential sources of bias or error. This helps ensure accurate and responsible data interpretation.

,

Honesty, Objectivity and Integrity

Honesty: Involves presenting information truthfully and without deception in all aspects of research, including data collection, analysis, and reporting .

Reliability: Refers to the consistency and dependability of research findings. Reliable research can be replicated and yields similar results under consistent conditions.

objectivity: Entails ensuring that personal biases, beliefs, or emotions do not influence the scientific process. It's about being transparent and allowing others to verify findings. impartiality and independence: Means conducting research without being influenced by external pressures or interests that could compromise the integrity of the research.

open communication: Involves sharing results and methodologies openly with the scientific community to allow for scrutiny, replication, and further advancement of knowledge.

Duty of care: Relates to the ethical treatment of research subjects, whether they are human participants or animals, ensuring their welfare and dignity.

Fairness: Encompasses giving proper credit for contributions to research, referencing work appropriately, and maintaining good relationships with colleagues.

Responsibility for Future Science Generations: Involves mentoring and supporting the development of future scientists, promoting ethical standards, and fostering an environment conducive to learning and growth.

In summary, these principles form the ethical compass guiding researchers toward meaningful, impactful, and responsible scientific endeavors. By adhering to these principles, we contribute to a better world where knowledge benefits all of society.

Scientific misconduct poses a significant threat to the integrity and credibility of research. It encompasses various unethical practices, such as data falsification, fabrication, plagiarism, and the intentional misrepresentation of findings. These actions not only undermine public trust in scientific inquiry but also impede the progress of genuine research efforts.

Preventing scientific misconduct requires a multifaceted approach. Adhering to rigorous ethical standards and guidelines, promoting transparency and accountability, and fostering a culture of integrity within research communities are crucial. Institutions must implement robust policies for detecting and addressing misconduct, while providing education and training to researchers on ethical research practices.

Chapter 3

Publication Ethics

When it comes to publishing research findings, authors, reviewers, and editors are guided by a set of rules and principles known as publication ethics. By ensuring that research is published truthfully, openly, and fairly, these principles uphold the integrity of the scientific record. Avoiding plagiarism by correctly crediting sources, making sure that each contributor receives the necessary credit for their work, declaring any conflicts of interest, and following strict peer review procedures are important components. Issues including data fabrication, falsification, and the appropriate management of retractions and corrections are also covered by publication ethics. Respecting these moral guidelines is crucial to increasing knowledge, encouraging confidence in scientific communication, and making sure that published findings can be consistently expanded upon.

3.1   Importance of Ethics

The collection of fundamental values, attitudes, and norms considered by most of the population as essential for personal life, life with one another, and life in relation to a society's institutions. Ethical transgressions can be considered to be misconduct.

Ethics is generally defined as a set of principles that distinguish between acceptable and unacceptable behavior or way of conducting a task. These guidelines or principles may vary across countries, disciplines, institutions, and even laboratories

3.2   What is Publication?

It is the dissemination of your findings to the scientific community. Scientific publications are subject to peer review. SCIENTIFIC PUBLICATION IS A TEAM EFFORT: Author–Reviewer–Journal–Publication

Researchers primarily use journal articles or books to communicate the results of their research to the scientific community and general public. Therefore, following publishing ethics is equally important for researchers and journals. Journals require authors to disclose whether the same research has been published before or is being considered for publication elsewhere. Duplicate publications and simultaneous submissions account for serious misconduct!

The different steps involved during publication include framing of the study design, conduction of the study, data collection and analysis, and finally drafting the article for publication. Ethical code of conduct is laid down for the researchers at all the steps. Committee on Publication Ethics (COPE) is an international platform for the editors and publishers of peer-reviewed journals providing the code of conduct and best practice guidelines related to publication ethics. Also, there exist guidelines for the editors on dealing with incidents of publication misconduct.

3.3   Publication Ethics

Publication ethics are rules of conduct generally agreed upon when publishing results of scientific research or other scholarly work. Generally, it is a standard that protects intellectual property and forbids the re-publication of another's work without proper credit. It also forbids the use of plagiarism of another's efforts. Data and information published as original must, in fact, be original.

Publication ethics came into play when Dr. Halvorson noticed a remarkable similarity in his work to another article published earlier.

Ethical standards for publication exist to ensure high-quality scientific publications, public trust in scientific findings, and that people receive credit for their work and ideas.

There are multiple steps in the publication cycle to be taken care of, one of which is considering ethical factors before submission of the manuscript.

- There are various forms of unethical practices that authors may resort to, sometimes intentionally and sometimes accidentally.

- Being aware of these publication ethics helps the authors to avoid such misconducts and submit honest and ethical publications.

- It prevents the article to be rejected and also saves the authors from embarrassments.

3.4   Ethics of Publications

Authorship is a serious decision and involves consideration of several factors. It is mandatory that researchers maintain daily log-books to record every days work and results. The records should be saved for inspection even years after publication. It should be understood that something being freely available on the internet does not mean that it can be copied as such. Due acknowledgment of web resources is an ethical practice. The authors must be aware of the issues of data/idea plagiarism and their consequences. Authors must follow honesty, objectivity and integrity and avoid bias in experimental design, data analysis, data interpretation, and reporting data, results, methods and procedures in all scientific communications.

The authors should be willing to share data, results, ideas, tools, and resources, especially after publication.

- It is the authors responsibility to honor patents, copyrights, and other forms of intellectual property.

- When privy to someone else's unpublished data/research plans (as a reviewer, editor or a visitor to a lab or member of audience at a lecture, etc.), it ought to be kept in mind that unauthorized use of such data and/or ideas for ones own work is unethical.

- It is mandatory for authors to be honest and objective when complying with journal submission requirements.

- Reuse of published data should follow rules regulating such usage.

- All communication between authors and the journal is to be treated as confidential.

3.5 Importance of Publication Ethics

Ethical standards are crucial to guarantee high quality of scientific distributions, credibility of scientific findings, and the respective authors duly receive credit for their work. ... Respect privacy of almost all stakeholders in the research and publications process.

Published research influences other researchers and establishes credibility for individual or journal. Honest scientific reports build trust among peers and within scientific community.

3.5.1 Data Fabrication and Falsification

Data fabrication means the researcher did not actually do the study but faked the data. Data falsification means the researcher did the experiment, but then changed some of the data.

3.5.2 Plagiarism

Taking the ideas and work of other scientists without giving them credit is unfair and dishonest. Copying even one sentence from someone elses manuscript, or even one of your own that has previously been published, without proper citation is considered plagiarism use your own words instead.

3.5.3 Multiple Submissions

It is unethical to submit the same manuscript to more than one journal at the same time. Doing this wastes the time of editors and peer reviewers and can damage the reputation of the authors and the journals if published in more than one journal as the later publication will have to be retracted.

3.5.4 Improper Author Contribution or Attribution

All listed authors must have made a significant scientific contribution to the research in the manuscript and approved all its claims. Dont forget to list everyone who made a significant scientific contribution, including students and laboratory technicians. Do not gift authorship to those who did not contribute to the paper. Many journals have tools and processes in place to identify researchers that engage in unethical behavior. If you are caught your manuscript may be rejected without review and your institution informed.

3.5.5   Redundant Publications (or Salami Publications)

This means publishing many very similar manuscripts based on the same experiment. Combining your results into one very robust paper is more likely to be of interest to a selective journal. Editors are likely to reject a weak paper that they suspect is a result of salami slicing.

3.6   General Ethical Principles

General ethical principles serve as foundational guidelines for behavior and decision-making across various contexts. Some key principles are:

Respect /Autonomy for persons: Individuals should be treated as autonomous agents. Persons with diminished autonomy are entitled to protection (Vulnerable population).

Beneficence: Maximizing benefits by promoting the well-being of subjects and society. This involves providing benefits and balancing them against potential risks and harms.

Justice: Persons bearing burden of research should receive appropriate benefits: subjects should not be placed at risk merely because of convenient access, their compromised position, or ability to be manipulated. This includes treating individuals equitably and without discrimination, and addressing inequalities and injustices.

Non-maleficence: Minimizing harm / No harm to the participant. This principle emphasizes the importance of not inflicting physical, emotional, or psychological harm.

Fidelity: Maintaining trust by being honest, keeping promises, and fulfilling commitments. This principle underscores the importance of integrity and reliability in professional and personal relationships.

Confidentiality: Protecting the privacy of information shared in a trusted relationship. This is particularly important in contexts like healthcare, counseling, and research.

Transparency: Being open and honest in communication, ensuring that all relevant information is disclosed and understood. This helps build trust and accountability.

Accountability: Taking responsibility for one's actions and decisions, and being willing to explain and justify them to others. This principle promotes ethical behavior and trustworthiness.

Respect for Persons: Treating every individual with dignity, valuing their inherent worth, and acknowledging their rights and perspectives.

Professionalism: Adhering to the ethical standards and practices of one's profession, demonstrating competence, and maintaining appropriate boundaries and conduct.

These principles provide a framework for ethical behavior, guiding individuals and organizations in making morally sound decisions and actions.

To sum up, publication ethics are essential to the advancement, legitimacy, and integrity of the scientific and academic domains. Reliability and trustworthiness of research findings are ensured by adhering to ethical principles such honesty, transparency, and fairness in authorship, peer review, and data reporting. Scholars and academic institutions can further knowledge and improve society at large by adhering to ethical publication procedures.

Chapter 4

Standards Setting Initiatives: COPE, WAME

Leading groups committed to promoting moral behaviour in academic and medical publishing include the Committee on Publication Ethics (COPE) and the World Association of Medical Editors (WAME). In order to help editors and publishers deal with ethical dilemmas including plagiarism, data fabrication, and conflicts of interest, COPE offers extensive guidelines and support. Through authorship, peer review, and editorial independence requirements, WAME aims to promote excellence in medical editing and publishing. In order to maintain the credibility, openness, and accountability of academic publications and guarantee reliable and morally sound research findings, COPE and WAME work together to perform critical roles.

4.1   Committee on Publication Ethics (COPE)

To address breaches of research and publication ethics, Cope was founded in 1997.

- A voluntary body providing a discussion forum and advice for scientific editors, it aims to find practical ways of dealing with the issues, and to develop good practice.

- Best practice in the ethics of scientific publishing guidelines should be useful for authors, editors, editorial board members, readers, owners of journals, and publishers.

- Intellectual honesty should be actively encouraged in all medical and scientific courses of study and used to inform publication ethics and prevent misconduct. It is with that in mind that these guidelines have been produced.

These guidelines are intended to be advisory rather than prescriptive, and to evolve over time. COPE (Committee on Publication Ethics) is committed to educating and supporting editors, publishers and those involved in publication ethics with the aim of moving the culture of publishing towards one where ethical practices become a normal part of the publishing culture.

Over 20 years, COPE has grown to support members worldwide, from all academic fields. COPE members are primarily editors, but also publishers and related organizations and individuals.

COPE provides advice to editors and publishers on all aspects of publication ethics and, in particular, how to handle cases of research and publication misconduct.

It also provides a forum for its members to discuss individual cases. COPE does not investigate individual cases but encourages editors to ensure that cases are investigated by the appropriate authorities (usually a research institution or employer).

All COPE members are expected to apply COPE principles of publication ethics outlined in the core practices.

4.1.1 Core Practices

Core practices are the policies and practices journals, and publishers need, to reach the highest standards in publication ethics. Each area includes cases with advice, guidance, education and events.

The Core Practices were developed in 2017, replacing the Code of Conduct. They are applicable to all involved in publishing scholarly literature: editors and their journals, publishers, and institutions.

The Core Practices should be considered alongside specific national and international codes of conduct for research and are not intended to replace these.

Journals and publishers should have robust and well described, publicly documented practices in all of the following areas for their journals:

i. **Allegations of Misconduct** Journals should have a clearly described process for handling allegations, however they are brought to the journals or publishers attention. Journals must take seriously allegations of misconduct pre-publication and post-publication. Policies should include how to handle allegations from whistleblowers.

ii. **Authorship and Contributorship** Clear policies (that allow for transparency around who contributed to the work and in what capacity) should be in place for requirements for authorship and contributorship as well as processes for managing potential disputes.

iii. **Complaints and Appeals** Journals should have a clearly described process for handling complaints against the journal, its staff, editorial board or publisher

iv. **Conflicts of interest / Competing interests** There must be clear definitions of conflicts of interest and processes for handling conflicts of interest of authors, reviewers, editors, journals and publishers, whether identified before or after publication

v. **Data and Reproducibility** Journals should include policies on data availability and encourage the use of reporting guidelines and registration of clinical trials and other study designs according to standard practice in their discipline

vi. **Ethical Oversight** Ethical oversight should include, but is not limited to, policies on consent to publication, publication on vulnerable populations, ethical conduct of research using animals, ethical conduct of research using human subjects, handling confidential data and ethical business/marketing practices

vii. **Intellectual Property** All policies on intellectual property, including copyright and publishing licenses, should be clearly described. In addition, any costs associated with publishing should be obvious to authors and readers.

Policies should be clear on what counts as prepublication that will preclude consideration. What constitutes plagiarism and redundant/overlapping publication should be specified.

viii. **Journal Management** A well-described and implemented infrastructure is essential, including the business model, policies, processes and software for efficient running of an editorially independent journal, as well as the efficient management and training of editorial boards and editorial and publishing staff

ix. **Peer Review Processes** All peer review processes must be transparently described and well managed.

Journals should provide training for editors and reviewers and have policies on diverse aspects of peer review, especially with respect to adoption of appropriate models of review and processes for handling conflicts of interest, appeals and disputes that may arise in peer review

x. **Post-publication Discussions and Corrections** Journals must allow debate post publication either on their site, through letters to the editor, or on an external moderated site, such as PubPeer. They must have mechanisms for correcting, revising or retracting articles after publication

COPE flowcharts can be found at: *https://publicationethics.org/guidance/Flowcharts*

4.2 WAME

WAME is a global nonprofit voluntary association of editors of peer-reviewed medical journals who seek to foster cooperation and communication among editors; improve editorial standards; promote professionalism in medical editing through education, self-criticism, and self-regulation; and encourage research on the principles and practice of medical editing.

WAME develops policies and recommendations of best practices for medical journal editors and has a syllabus for editors that members are encouraged to follow. Journals' reputations depend on the trust of readers, authors, researchers, reviewers, editors, patients, research subjects, funding agencies, and administrators of public health policy. This trust is enhanced by describing as explicitly as possible the journal's policies to ensure the ethical treatment of all participants in the publication process.

Every journal should have an explicit policy on each of these issues, and that these policies should be published in each journal, so they are accessible to readers, authors, and reviewers.

Recommendations on...

- Conflict of Interest in Peer-Reviewed Medical Journals

- Study Design and Ethics

- Authorship

- Peer Review

- Editorial Decisions

- Originality, Prior Publication, and Media Relations

- Plagiarism

- Advertising

- Responding to Allegations of Possible Misconduct

- Relation of the Journal to the Sponsoring Society (if applicable)

4.2.1 WAME Policies

The World Association of Medical Editors (WAME) provides a comprehensive set of policies and guidelines designed to promote ethical practices in medical editing and publishing. Here are some key policies:

Conflict of Interest: WAME emphasizes the importance of disclosing conflicts of interest to maintain transparency and trust. Editors, authors, and reviewers are required to disclose any financial or personal relationships that could influence their work.

Authorship Criteria: WAME provides guidelines to ensure that authorship is attributed fairly and accurately. This includes requiring substantial contributions to the conception, design, execution, or interpretation of the research, drafting or revising the article, and approving the final version for publication.

Peer Review Process: WAME supports a rigorous and unbiased peer review process. Editors are encouraged to ensure that reviewers are independent and that the process is conducted confidentially to maintain the integrity of the review.

Research Misconduct: WAME advocates for strict policies to address research misconduct, including plagiarism, data fabrication, and falsification. Journals are encouraged to investigate allegations thoroughly and take appropriate action when misconduct is confirmed.

Editorial Independence: WAME underscores the importance of editorial independence, ensuring that editors can make decisions based on the quality and relevance of the submissions without undue influence from publishers, sponsors, or other stakeholders.

Ethical Research: WAME promotes the ethical conduct of research involving human and animal subjects. This includes adhering to relevant ethical guidelines and ensuring that all necessary approvals and consents have been obtained.

Transparency in Reporting: WAME encourages journals to adopt policies that require complete and transparent reporting of research methods and findings. This helps ensure the reproducibility and reliability of published research.

Data Sharing: WAME supports policies that promote data sharing and openness. Researchers are encouraged to make their data available to others for verification and further study, while respecting privacy and confidentiality concerns.

Corrections and Retractions: WAME advocates for clear policies on issuing corrections, retractions, and expressions of concern to address errors or ethical issues in published articles. This helps maintain the accuracy and integrity of the scientific record.

Diversity and Inclusivity: WAME encourages journals to promote diversity and inclusivity in their editorial practices, including the selection of reviewers and editorial board members, and to address biases that may affect the publication process.

These policies help ensure that medical journals operate with integrity, transparency, and accountability, fostering trust and credibility in the medical literature (*https://www.wame.org/policies*).

To sum up, the World Association of Medical Editors (WAME) and the Committee on Publication Ethics (COPE) are essential to preserving the moral principles and integrity of academic and medical publication. These organizations guarantee responsible and transparent research conduct and dissemination by offering editors, authors, and reviewers comprehensive guidelines, resources, and support. The legitimacy and dependability of scholarly and medical writings are greatly increased by their attempts to resolve ethical problems including plagiarism, conflicts of interest, and research misconduct. Respecting the values outlined by WAME and COPE is crucial for scientific advancement, building public confidence, and assisting the ethical growth of the international research community.

Chapter 5

Conflict Of Interest (COI)

Conflict of interest in publication occurs when there is a situation in which the judgment or actions of individuals involved in the publication process could be influenced by personal, financial, or other interests that could potentially undermine the objectivity, integrity, or credibility of the research or publication.

- Conflicts or competing of interest (COI) include financial, personal, social, or other factors that directly or indirectly influence the decision of the particular manuscript under consideration. Failure to disclose such hidden interests severely affects the outcome.

- Direct conflict of interest occurs when the author is an employee, a supplier, or own patent of the product such as drug, or device highlighted in the article.

- Indirect conflict arises when the author receives any honorarium or research grant. Personal interests could be due to being a friend, family member, or relative of the author or co-authors or due to the same ideology or thought process following political or religious reasons.

COI does not always stop work from being published or prevent someone from being involved in the review process. However, they must be declared.

If COI are detected after publication of the article, this may be embarrassing for the authors and may require a corrigendum or reassessment of the review process.

Authors and reviewers should declare all COI relevant to the work under consideration (i.e., relationships, both financial and personal, that might interfere with the interpretation of the work) or may lead to any bias.

The changing dynamics of research environment and collaborations can often give rise to conflicts of interests and commitments/obligations. Therefore, it is important to maintain transparency in research and publication by both authors and publishers.

5.1   What Constitutes Conflicts of Interest?

For instance, conflicts of interest can arise when a researcher who is heading the research of a product is also a visiting consultant at the parent company.

Conflicts of interest can also arise when an author, researcher, editor, or a peer reviewer has a relationship (personal or financial) that can directly or indirectly affect his/her objectivity in making decisions or influence his/her actions.

COI can arise at various stages, involving authors, reviewers, editors, and even institutions. Here's a more detailed elaboration on different aspects of conflict of interest in publication:

i. **Authors:**

   Financial relationships: This is one of the most common types of conflicts of interest. It occurs when researchers, authors, reviewers, or editors have financial relationships (such as employment, consulting fees, stock ownership, or patent interests) with organizations that could potentially benefit or be affected by the research outcomes. For example, a researcher working on a clinical trial funded by a pharmaceutical company may have financial incentives tied to the study's outcome.

   Personal relationships: Conflicts of interest can also arise from personal relationships, including familial or romantic relationships, close friendships, rivalry or academic/professional mentor-ship. These relationships could influence decisions on manuscript acceptance, peer review, or funding allocation.

   Intellectual beliefs: Sometimes conflicts of interest can be intellectual or ideological, where individuals have strong personal beliefs, academic biases, or preconceived notions that could impact their objectivity in assessing research or making editorial decisions.

   Academic competition: It can include biased judgements because of the direct or indirect competition with peers or colleagues.

   Professional conflicts: Individuals involved in the publication process may have professional conflicts of interest stemming from their institutional affiliations, academic positions, or career advancement interests. For instance, editors or reviewers affiliated with competing institutions might have biases that affect their evaluation of a manuscript.

ii. **Reviewers:** Reviewers are expected to provide impartial evaluations of manuscripts. However, COI can arise if a reviewer has personal or professional relationships with the authors, competitive interests in the research topic, or has previously collaborated closely with the authors.

iii. **Editors:** Editors play a crucial role in deciding whether to accept or reject manuscripts for publication. COI for editors may involve personal relationships with authors, financial interests in the outcomes of published research, or institutional pressures to favor certain research agendas.

iv. **Institutions and Funding Agencies:** Institutions and funding agencies may also face COI situations, particularly when they have financial stakes in research outcomes or when their policies or reputations are affected by published research.

5.1.1 Impacts of COI

Conflict of interest (COI) poses serious risks across the research and publication landscape, impacting various facets of scientific integrity and public trust. COI can indeed lead to biased research findings, where financial or personal interests influence study design, data interpretation, and the reporting of results. This selective reporting can skew the presentation of research outcomes, potentially distorting scientific understanding and undermining the reliability of published findings. Furthermore, COI may exert undue influence on editorial decisions, affecting the selection, peer review process, and publication of manuscripts. Such influence can compromise the objectivity and rigor expected in scholarly publishing.

Failure to disclose COI represents a critical ethical breach that can have far-reaching consequences. It undermines transparency and accountability in research, depriving readers, reviewers, and policymakers of crucial information needed to assess the reliability and impartiality of research findings. In severe cases, undisclosed COI can lead to retractions of published papers, damaging the credibility of authors, journals, and institutions involved. Moreover, it erodes public trust in scientific integrity, potentially jeopardizing public confidence in research outcomes and the effectiveness of regulatory and policy decisions based on that research.

Addressing COI requires robust policies, stringent disclosure requirements, and ethical oversight mechanisms to ensure transparency and mitigate its impact on research quality and credibility. By promoting responsible conduct and upholding rigorous ethical standards, stakeholders can uphold the integrity of scientific inquiry, foster public trust, and safeguard the credibility of scholarly communication.

5.2 Management and Disclosure

Managing conflicts of interest is crucial for maintaining the integrity and credibility of scholarly publications. Most academic journals and publishing platforms require authors, reviewers, and editors to disclose any potential conflicts of interest.

Disclosure of COI is a critical step in managing potential biases. Authors, reviewers, and editors are typically required to disclose any relevant COI at the submission stage or during the review process. Disclosure of potential conflicts of interest is essential in scholarly publishing to maintain transparency and trust. It allows readers, reviewers, and editors to assess any potential biases and ensures that decisions related to the research and publication are made impartially and ethically.

Journals and institutions often have policies and guidelines in place to manage COI, including mechanisms for handling conflicts, transparent reporting, and independent review processes.

To address conflicts of interest effectively, journals may implement policies such as:

- **Disclosure Requirements:** Authors, reviewers, and editors must disclose any financial or non-financial relationships that could influence their work.

- **Independent Review:** Reviewers and editors should be impartial and may recluse themselves from handling manuscripts where a conflict of interest exists.

- **Transparency:** Journals often include conflict of interest statements in published articles, outlining any declared conflicts and how they were managed during the publication process.

In general, addressing conflicts of interest in publications requires openness and moral behaviour in order to preserve academic integrity standards and guarantee the validity of the distribution of scientific knowledge.

In conclusion, conflicts of interest in publications are a complicated ethical problem that need to be handled carefully to maintain the reliability and integrity of academic research. In order to reduce the dangers related to conflict of interest (COI) and preserve the legitimacy of academic publishing, transparency, disclosure, and adherence to ethical standards are crucial.

Chapter 6

Publication Misconduct

Publication misconduct refers to unethical practices or behaviors that undermine the integrity of scholarly publishing. These actions violate ethical standards and can include various forms of misconduct that distort, manipulate, or misrepresent research findings.

6.1 Definition of Misconduct

The US Office of Research Integrity defines misconduct quite narrowly as: "...fabrication, falsification, or plagiarism in proposing, performing or reviewing research, or in reporting research results".

Others have used broader definitions, for example Nylenna & Simonsen wrote:

" Scientific misconduct...is a continuum ranging from honest errors to outright fraud...The research community must take a collective responsibility even for its deviants... Moving the whole research community in the right direction should reduce the number of serious cases." The Lancet, 367, 1882, 1884, 2006.

Research Misconduct

- Fabrication (making up data or results)

- Falsification (manipulating research materials, or changing or omitting data or results)

- Plagiarism (appropriation of another's ideas)

- Not honest error or differences of opinion

Other Types of Publication Misconduct

It may be duplicate publication, self-plagiarism, faked author approval, and other ethical violations. Here are some key types of publication misconduct:

Fabrication:

Inventing or falsifying research data, results, or experimental procedures. Fabrication can involve creating data that does not exist or manipulating data to support desired conclusions.

Falsification of data:

Manipulating research materials, equipment, or processes, or changing or omitting data or results such that the research is not accurately represented in the publication.

Plagiarism:

Presenting someone else's work, ideas, or words as one's own without appropriate acknowledgment. This includes both verbatim copying and paraphrasing without proper citation.

Problematic data presentation or analysis.

Failure to obtain ethical approval by the Research Ethics Committee or to obtain the subject's informed consent.

Inappropriate claims of authorship:

Improper assignment of authorship credit, including including individuals who have not significantly contributed to the research or excluding those who have made substantial contributions.

Duplicate publication:

Publishing the same or very similar research findings in more than one journal without proper cross-referencing or justification. This can include submitting identical manuscripts to different journals simultaneously.

Undisclosed conflict of interest (COI):

Failing to disclose financial, personal, or professional conflicts of interest that could influence the research or its publication. COI violations can bias research findings or editorial decisions.

In the era of 'publish or perish' medical fraternity should not focus only on his/her career advancement but also consider the professional ethics including research and publication ethics seriously. E.g. Hwang's revolutionary work on stem cells published in Science (2004 and 2005) and later found that both the papers are fake.

According to Fanelli, Research misconduct should be redefined as "any omission or misrepresentation of the information necessary and sufficient to evaluate the validity and significance of research, at the level appropriate to the context in which the research is communicated".

6.1.1   Reasons for More Misconduct and Unethical Behaviour?

Several factors contribute to the rise in misconduct and unethical behavior in research and publication:

Lack of Knowledge about Research and Publication Ethics:

Many researchers, particularly early-career ones, may not receive adequate training or guidance on research ethics and publication practices.

Without clear understanding and adherence to ethical norms, researchers may unintentionally or negligently engage in practices like improper data handling, plagiarism, or inaccurate reporting.

Larger, Multi-disciplinary, and Global Collaborations:

Collaborative research involving multiple disciplines and institutions across different countries can present challenges in maintaining consistent ethical standards.

Differences in ethical norms, cultural practices, and regulatory frameworks may lead to misunderstandings or disagreements regarding ethical conduct and reporting standards.

Increasing Pressure on Researchers to Publish:

The "publish or perish" culture places significant pressure on researchers to publish frequently and in high-impact journals to advance their careers and secure funding.

This pressure can incentivize shortcuts or compromises in ethical standards, such as selective reporting of results or rushing through peer review processes.

Financial Inducements Compromising Integrity:

Financial incentives, such as bonuses or promotions tied to publication metrics, can create conflicts of interest and compromise research integrity.

Researchers may be tempted to prioritize quantity over quality, engage in guest authorship to boost publication records, or succumb to pressure from sponsors or funders to produce favorable results.

Addressing these challenges requires concerted efforts from institutions, funders, publishers, and researchers themselves. It involves promoting education on research ethics, fostering a culture of integrity and transparency, establishing clear guidelines and oversight mechanisms, and incentivizing responsible research practices over sheer productivity. By addressing these underlying factors, the research community can mitigate the incidence of misconduct and uphold the credibility and reliability of scientific research and publication.

6.2   How Common is Misconduct?

Systematic Review and meta-analysis on fabrication and falsification of results (Fanelli 2009): 2 % admitted to fabrication, falsification or manipulation of results, 14% reported witnessing this behavior in a colleague. 67.4% of retractions due to misconduct (Fang et al. 2012), Fraud 43.3%, duplicate publication 14.2%, plagiarism 9.8%. Estimates on prevalence of plagiarism in submitted manuscripts vary, One Chinese journal found 'unreasonable degrees of copying' in 22.8% of submitted manuscripts.

Graf et al said that academic publishing depends mainly on 'trust'. Scientists are generally perceived as well-intentioned seekers of truth; universities, as cathedrals of learning and as producers of knowledge vital to the health and welfare of society. World Association of Medical Editors (WAME), International Committee of Medical Journal Editors (ICMJE) and Committee on Publication Ethics (COPE) are the guiding force to interpret ethical publication appropriately.

The Committee on Publication Ethics (COPE) has outlined guidelines for journal editors to identify and avoid such misconducts in submitted manuscripts and published papers. Researchers should consider the following points to avoid unethical publishing practices:

- Do not submit the same paper to different journals.

- Maintain transparency during submission and peer review process on previously published work (disclose publication in conference proceedings, submission to a pre-print repository etc.).

- Check with the publisher about translating and publishing the work again.

- Disclose already published and/or translated versions of the submitted manuscript.

- Avoid dividing your study into multiple publications.

6.2.1   Compulsions to Indulge in Such Unethical Practices

Desire to see voluminous curriculum vitae, to increase number of publications for promotions and academic advancement, overinflated bibliography is also utilized for grant sanctioning, competition among the colleagues, to prove professional supremacy and in many universities, publications are the criteria to become guide/internal or external-examiners

Ph.D. candidates and Masters level students, who by force of educational rules, are required to publish articles during their educational courses and long for non-scientific ways to lead the rest of their lives, are among other victims of some erroneous policies forcing them to write papers as a demanding job.

This, indeed, pushes them towards disregard for legal frameworks of publication ethics

6.2.2   What is the Harm?

Publication misconduct can have serious and far-reaching consequences, undermining the integrity of scientific research and public trust. Here's an elaboration on the key harms associated with such misconduct:

i. **Distraction from truth**
   Publication misconduct detracts from accurate and true scientific discoveries, such as the fabrication of data.

   Misleading Conclusions: False data releases have the potential to provide inaccurate findings and theories that serve as a roadblock for further research.

   Resource Wastage: The pursuit of valid scientific discoveries may be slowed down by scientists squandering important time, funds, and resources in an effort to corroborate or expand on false findings.

ii. **Adoption of ineffective or harmful interventions**
   Adoption of inefficient or even dangerous interventions can occur when medical guidelines or public health policy are influenced by false or biassed research.

Patient Harm: When clinical decisions are made based on erroneous information, patients may suffer unnecessarily, experience negative side effects, or receive inadequate care.

Public Health Risks: When public health treatments are implemented based on inaccurate data, diseases may not be properly controlled, which could lead to worse public health outcomes.

iii. **Damaged reputations**
Publication misconduct can severely damage the reputations of individuals, institutions, and the broader scientific community.

Personal Consequences: Researchers found guilty of misconduct may face career-ending repercussions, including loss of credibility, job termination, and legal consequences.

Institutional Trust: Institutions associated with misconduct may suffer damage to their reputations, losing trust from funders, collaborators, and the public.

iv. **Sensationalism in news media**
Publication misconduct can contribute to sensationalism in the news media, where inaccurate or exaggerated findings are reported.

Public Misperception: Sensationalized news based on fraudulent research can misinform the public, leading to widespread misconceptions about scientific facts and health information.

Policy Influence: Misleading media reports can influence policy decisions, leading to ineffective or harmful regulations and interventions.

v. **Erosion of trust in research**
Repeated instances of publication misconduct contribute to a general erosion of trust in the research community and scientific findings.

Public Skepticism: The public may become skeptical of scientific research, questioning the validity of genuine findings and the integrity of researchers.

Funding Challenges: Erosion of trust can make it more difficult to secure funding for legitimate research, as funders may become wary of investing in potentially fraudulent projects.

Collaboration Barriers: International and interdisciplinary collaborations may be hindered by trust issues, reducing the overall effectiveness and innovation potential in research.

6.2.3 What Can be Done?

Addressing publication misconduct requires proactive measures to identify and mitigate the impact of tainted articles. Here are key actions that can be taken:

Identifying Tainted Articles

Establishing robust mechanisms for detecting publication misconduct, such as systematic screening for plagiarism, data fabrication, and falsification. Utilizing tools and technologies to scan published literature and flag potential instances of misconduct.

Retracting Fraudulent Articles

Promptly retracting articles found to contain fraudulent data or findings. Implementing clear policies and procedures for retracting articles, ensuring transparency in the retraction process.

Improving Retraction Processes

Reducing the time to retract fraudulent articles to minimize their impact on the scientific community and public trust. Increasing awareness of retractions among researchers and the public, ensuring that retractions are prominently displayed and easily accessible in academic databases.

Preventing Citation of Fraudulent Research

Educating researchers, reviewers, and editors about the importance of verifying the integrity of research before citing it. Developing tools and databases that flag retracted articles to prevent their unintentional citation in future research.

Promoting Ethical Practices

Encouraging adherence to ethical guidelines and best practices in research and publication. Providing training and resources to researchers and editors on ethical conduct and responsible publication practices.

Collaborative Efforts

Collaborating with academic institutions, funding agencies, and publishers to develop and enforce standards for publication ethics. Establishing networks and platforms for sharing information about publication misconduct and best practices for addressing it.

By implementing these measures, the scientific community can mitigate the impact of publication misconduct, uphold the integrity of research, and maintain public trust in scientific findings. These efforts contribute to a more transparent and reliable scholarly publishing environment.

6.3   COPE Core Practices

Core practices are the essential policies and procedures that journals and publishers must follow to achieve the highest standards in publication ethics. COPE provide case studies, practical advice, guidance for daily operations, as well as educational modules and events on current topics to help journals and publishers implement their policies effectively (https://publicationethics.org):

"Journals must take seriously allegations of misconduct pre-publication and post-publication".

"Journals should have a clearly described process for handling allegations, however they are brought to the journal's or publisher's attention".

"COPE expects members to have robust and well-described, publicly documented practices in all these areas for their journals and organizations".

"Editors are accountable and should take responsibility for everything they publish".

"Editors should pursue reviewer and editorial misconduct".

"Editors should guard the integrity of the published record by issuing corrections and retractions when needed and pursuing suspected or alleged research and publication misconduct".

"Editors should have appropriate policies in place for handling editorial conflicts of interest".

6.4 Violation of Publication Ethics

Violation of publication ethics is a global problem which includes duplicate submission, multiple submissions, plagiarism, gift authorship, fake affiliation, ghost authorship, pressured authorship, salami publication and fraud (fabrication and falsification) but excludes the honest errors committed by the authors.

Data Fabrication and Falsification: "Data fabrication means the researcher did not actually do the study but made-up data. Data falsification means the researcher did the experiment, but then changed some of the data. Both of these practices make people distrust scientists. If the public is mistrustful of science, then it will be less willing to provide funding support".

Plagiarism: "In an instructional setting, plagiarism occurs when a writer deliberately uses someone else's language, ideas, or other original (not common-knowledge) material without acknowledging its source." Students plagiarize in four main ways:

1. Stealing material from another source and passing it off as their own.

2. Submitting a paper written by someone else (e.g., a peer or relative) and passing it off as their own.

3. Copying sections of material from one or more source texts, supplying proper documentation (including the full reference) but leaving out quotation marks, thus giving the impression that the material has been paraphrased rather than directly quoted.

4. Paraphrasing material from one or more source texts without supplying appropriate documentation.

Multiple submissions of a paper: "It is unethical to submit the same manuscript to more than one journal at the same time. This is also a waste of time for editors and peer reviewers and can give rise to prejudices at the reputation of journals if published in more than one".

Redundant publications (or 'salami' publications): "This means publishing many very similar manuscripts based on the same experiment. It can make readers less likely to pay attention to your manuscripts".

Improper author contribution or attribution: "All listed authors must have made a significant scientific contribution to the research in the manuscript and approved all its claims. Don't forget to list everyone who made a significant scientific contribution".

Publication misconduct undermines the reliability and credibility of scientific literature, hinders scientific progress, and damages the reputation of researchers, institutions, and journals involved. To uphold the integrity of scholarly publishing, it is essential for authors, reviewers, editors, and institutions to adhere strictly to ethical guidelines, disclose potential conflicts of interest, and maintain transparency in all aspects of research and publication.

6.5 Identification of Publication Misconduct

Publication misconduct includes plagiarism, fabrication, falsification, inappropriate authorship, duplicate submission/multiple submissions, overlapping publication, and salami publication.

"Breach of Publication Ethics" is a much lesser indiscretion than "misconduct" and includes a variety of items such as failure to reveal a financial conflict of interest; redundant publication (also referred to as "fragmented, prior, dual, double, duplicate, or repetitive publications");adding a non-contributing author or omitting a deserving author; misrepresenting the status of a publication in the references, such as claiming that a paper is "in press"; and self-plagiarism without attribution.

The self-plagiarism issue is controversial, but authors should realize that they may have transferred the copyright (ownership) of their previously published material to a publisher. Journals are not investigative bodies, and their editors must decide how to handle allegations of misconduct or ethical breaches

6.6 Actions for Misconduct

There are clear guidelines on steps to be taken by the Editorial team when each of the above-mentioned misconduct is detected.

- It may include in contacting the authors and informing them that their misconduct has been identified.

- If the authors acknowledge and accept their fault, the paper may be rejected and the higher authorities in the authors' institution be informed.

- If the paper is already published, authors are provided with an opportunity of self-confession in the form of an erratum in the journal.

- If the misconduct is major and confirmed, then the editor has the right to revoke the paper and the authors can be blacklisted by the journal. Also, this information can be passed on to COPE so that all the other member journals are also informed about the misdeed of the authors and co-authors.

If authors deny their misconduct, editors can take cognizance and appropriate action as per the guidelines set forth. Authors can be questioned by the ethics committee of their institutions and suitable punishment can be handed out as per the standard operating procedures laid down by them. At the time of submitting a manuscript most journals seek a written undertaking from the authors that the manuscript is original, not being considered for publication by any other scientific journal and has been approved by all co-authors and responsible authorities at the concerned institute or organization. Even it should be stated that the order of authorship has been consented by all concerned.

6.7 Dealing With Possible Misconduct

The editor has a duty to act if he/she suspect misconduct or if an allegation of misconduct is brought to him. This duty extends to both published and unpublished papers.

- The editor should not simply reject papers that raise concerns about possible misconduct. He/she is ethically obliged to pursue alleged cases.

- The editor should follow the COPE flowcharts where applicable (https://publicationethics.org/guidance/Flowcharts).

- The editor should first seek a response from those suspected of misconduct. If he/she is not satisfied with the response, he/she should ask the relevant employers, or institution, or some appropriate body (perhaps a regulatory body or national research integrity organization) to investigate.

- The editor should make all reasonable efforts to ensure that a proper investigation into alleged misconduct is conducted; if this does not happen, the editor should make all reasonable attempts to persist in obtaining a resolution to the problem. This is an onerous but important duty.

- Journals must take seriously allegations of misconduct pre-publication and post-publication.

- "Journals should have a clearly described process for handling allegations, however they are brought to the journal's or publisher's attention"

- "COPE expects members to have robust and well-described, publicly documented practices in all these areas for their journals and organisations"

The current Core Practices and flowcharts can be found on the COPE website and should be considered alongside specific national and international codes of conduct for research and is not intended to replace them.

To sum up, publication misconduct poses a serious threat to the reliability and integrity of scientific research. The foundation of scientific publishing is undermined by instances of fraud, plagiarism, and unethical behaviours, which may mislead the public, policymakers, and researchers. Vigilant oversight, explicit procedures for identifying and withdrawing fraudulent articles, and initiatives to stop the citation of tainted research are all necessary to address publishing misconduct. By encouraging openness, moral conduct, and responsibility at every stage of the study and publishing process, the scientific community can maintain the validity of results that are published, cultivate confidence among interested parties, and guarantee that scientific advancements are founded on a strong and reliable basis. This dedication is necessary to further knowledge, uphold academic integrity, and eventually serve society at large.

Chapter 7

Authorship

Authorship in scholarly publishing refers to the designation of individuals who have made substantial intellectual contributions to a research study or manuscript and who therefore share responsibility and credit for the work.

7.1 Key Principles

Authorship is a critical aspect of academic integrity and ethical practice in research, and it typically entails the following key principles and considerations:

1. *Substantial Contributions:* Authors are individuals who have made significant contributions to the conception, design, execution, or interpretation of the research study. This may include planning experiments, collecting and analyzing data, drafting or critically revising the manuscript, and approving the final version for submission.

2. *Intellectual Content:* Authorship is based on intellectual contributions rather than on other roles, such as providing funding, supervising the research, or providing access to resources, unless these activities also involve substantial intellectual input.

3. *Criteria for Authorship:* The International Committee of Medical Journal Editors (ICMJE) has established widely accepted criteria for authorship, often referred to as the "ICMJE criteria." According to these criteria, authors should meet all of the following conditions:

   i. Substantial contributions to the conception or design of the work; or the acquisition, analysis, or interpretation of data for the work; AND

   ii. Drafting the work or revising it critically for important intellectual content; AND

   iii. Final approval of the version to be published; AND

   iv. Agreement to be accountable for all aspects of the work in ensuring that questions related to the accuracy or integrity of any part of the work are appropriately investigated and resolved.

4. *Order of Authors:* The order of authors typically reflects the relative contributions of each individual to the research. The first author is often the individual who made the

most substantial contributions and led the research effort, while subsequent authors are listed based on their contributions, with the last author often being the senior researcher who supervised the project.

5. *Contributorship vs. Acknowledgments:* Individuals who do not meet the criteria for authorship but have contributed to the research in other ways (e.g., technical support, data collection assistance) should be acknowledged in the manuscript's acknowledgments section rather than listed as authors.

6. *Disputes and Resolutions:* Authorship disputes can arise due to disagreements over contributions or other issues. It is essential for research teams to establish clear guidelines and agreements regarding authorship early in the research process and to resolve any disputes through open communication and adherence to ethical guidelines.

7.2 Author Misconduct

Author misconduct refers to unethical or inappropriate behaviors by researchers or authors that undermine the integrity and reliability of scholarly publications. Such misconduct can have serious consequences for the credibility of research findings and the academic community as a whole.

7.2.1 Types of Author Misconduct

Three major types of author misconduct include ghost, gifted, or guest authorships.

1. *Ghost authors* are usually paid authors who contribute substantially towards the making of the paper but are not included in the authorship list nor are acknowledged in the submitted manuscript.

2. *Gift authorship* refers to those included in the list of authors simply due to an affiliation to an institute where the research was conducted. It is usually implied for heads of departments or institution even without their contribution to the study.

3. *Guest authorship* is usually provided to individuals whose presence as one of the author significantly improves the chances of acceptance of the manuscript.

Changes in the list of authors either as addition or removal after acceptance or sometimes after publication can be considered only if all the coauthors agree to this amendment and have individually signed the requisition sent to the editorial office.

It is at the discretion of the Editor-in-Chief to accept or reject their requests depending on the merit of the case.

7.3 Contributorship

Contributorship refers to the roles and responsibilities individuals have in the research process, particularly in the context of scholarly publications. It encompasses the specific contributions made by individuals to a research project or manuscript, regardless of whether they meet the criteria for authorship. Understanding contributorship is essential for transparency, accountability, and proper recognition of everyone involved in producing research outputs.

7.3.1 Contributorship Eligibility

An individual having a role in the research is eligible to be a contributor. Contributorship **includes authorship as well as those contributions**, which do not qualify as authorship. Therefore, it is imperative that the exact contribution of each individual is described in detail whether it amounts to authorship or not.

Contributorship delineates the roles and responsibilities of individuals who contribute to different aspects of a research project or manuscript. It goes beyond authorship to acknowledge all significant contributions, including but not limited to data collection, analysis, methodology design, drafting, reviewing, and funding acquisition.

- Intellectual (ideas, writing)

- Practical (conducting research, data analysis)

- Financial (funds, experimental material)

Authorship typically follows specific criteria (e.g., ICMJE criteria) and involves those who have made substantial intellectual contributions to the research and manuscript. In contrast, contributorship acknowledges a broader range of contributions that may not meet the criteria for authorship but are nevertheless essential to the research process.

When a multicenter group has carried out the research, the group should identify the individuals who accept direct responsibility for each part of the work. These individuals should completely meet the criteria for authorship/ contributorship.

General supervision of the research group alone, acquisition of funding, or data collection does not constitute authorship.

All persons who contribute to the study and do not meet the criteria for authorship should be listed in the Acknowledgments; including a department chairperson who provided only general support and persons who provided purely technical help or writing assistance.

Contributors may include researchers, technicians, statisticians, database managers, administrative support staff, and others who have contributed intellectually or logistically to the research project. Each contributor's role should be clearly defined and acknowledged.These persons must give written permission to be acknowledged, because readers may argue their endorsement of the data and conclusions. Recognizing contributorship promotes fairness and transparency in research. It helps prevent disputes over authorship and ensures that all individuals who have contributed significantly to the research receive appropriate credit and recognition.

The corresponding author is responsible for providing the contributions of all authors at the time of submission. It is expected that all authors will have reviewed, discussed, and agreed to their contributions ahead of this time. Contributions will be published with the final article, and they should accurately reflect contributions to the work.

Many journals and publishers have policies or guidelines regarding contributorship and require authors to disclose each contributor's roles and contributions. This practice sup-

Contributor Role	Role Definition
Conceptualization	Ideas formulation or evolution of overarching research goals and aims
Data Curation	Management activities to annotate (produce metadata), scrub data and maintain research data (including software code, where it is necessary for interpreting the data itself) for initial use and later reuse.
Formal Analysis	Application of statistical, mathematical, computational, or other formal techniques to analyze or synthesize study data.
Funding Acquisition	Acquisition of the financial support for the project leading to this publication.
Investigation	Conducting a research and investigation process, specifically performing the experiments, or data/evidence collection.
Methodology	Development or design of methodology; creation of models
Project Administration	Management and coordination responsibility for the research activity planning and execution.
Resources	Provision of study materials, reagents, materials, patients, laboratory samples, animals, instrumentation, computing resources, or other analysis tools.
Software	Programming, software development; designing computer programs; implementation of the computer code and supporting algorithms; testing of existing code components.
Supervision	Oversight and leadership responsibility for the research activity planning and execution, including mentorship external to the core team.
Validation	Verification, whether as a part of the activity or separate, of the overall replication/reproducibility of results/experiments and other research outputs.
Visualization	Preparation, creation and/or presentation of the published work, specifically visualization/data presentation.
Writing- Original Draft Preparation	Creation and/or presentation of the published work, specifically writing Draft Preparation the initial draft (including substantive translation).
Writing- Review and Editing	Preparation, creation and/or presentation of the published work by those from the original research group, specifically critical review, commentary or revision – including pre- or post-publication stages.

Table 7.1: Contributor Role Definition

ports ethical publishing standards and helps maintain the integrity of scholarly communication. Various contributor roles and their role definitions are given in Table 7.1.

Many journals now require or encourage authors to provide detailed contributorship statements that specify the roles of each contributor in the research. These statements help clarify who did what in the study and ensure proper credit is given to all individuals involved.

Institutions and funding agencies are increasingly emphasizing the importance of contributorship. They encourage researchers to adopt clear guidelines and practices for acknowledging contributions, thereby promoting good research practices and ethical conduct.

To sum up, authorship in scholarly and academic publications is an important factor that represents contributions to research and scholarly labour. Appropriate rules and moral principles for authorship contribute to the preservation of accountability, fairness, and transparency in the academic community. All persons who have contributed significantly intellectually to a study must be duly credited as authors; those who do not fit these requirements should be acknowledged in some other way, such as the acknowledgments section. Respecting these guidelines encourages cooperation, trust, and integrity in academic research in addition to ensuring that contributors receive due credit. Researchers can enhance the legitimacy of published work and promote significant advancements in knowledge and innovation across disciplines by upholding strict authorship criteria.

Chapter 8

Complaints and Appeals

Complaints and appeals are crucial mechanisms in scholarly publishing to address issues related to the publication process, ensure transparency, and maintain the integrity of the academic record. These mechanisms allow authors, reviewers, and readers to raise concerns and seek resolutions when they believe that errors, unfair practices, or ethical breaches have occurred.

8.1   Who Complains or Makes an Appeal?

Submitters, authors, reviewers, and readers may register complaints and appeals in a variety of cases as follows: falsification, fabrication, plagiarism, duplicate publication, authorship dispute, conflict of interest, ethical treatment of animals, informed consent, bias or unfair inappropriate competitive acts, copyright, stolen data, defamation, and legal problem.

If any individuals or institutions want to inform the cases, they can send a letter to editor. For the complaints or appeals, concrete data with answers to all factual questions (who, when, where, what, how, why) should be provided.

8.1.1   Types of Complaints

Various aspects of complaints and appeals in publication are:

Editorial Decisions: Complaints regarding rejection of manuscripts, perceived bias, or unfair treatment during the peer review process.

Publication Ethics: Concerns about plagiarism, authorship disputes, data fabrication or falsification, and other ethical violations.

Process and Communication: Issues related to delays in the publication process, lack of transparency in editorial decisions, or poor communication from the journal.

Content Issues: Errors in published articles, such as factual inaccuracies, misleading data, or inappropriate content.

8.1.2 Appeals

Journals should consider establishing and publishing a mechanism for authors to appeal editorial decisions, to facilitate genuine appeals, and to discourage repeated or unfounded appeals.

Editors should allow appeals to override earlier decisions only when new information becomes available (for example, additional factual input by the authors, revisions, extra material in the manuscript, or appeals about conflicts of interest and concerns about biased peer review). Author protest alone should not affect decisions. Reversals of decisions without new evidence should be avoided.

Editors should mediate all exchanges between authors and peer reviewers during the peer-review process. Editors may seek comments from additional peer reviewers to help them make their final decision.

Journals should state in their guidelines that the editor's decision following an appeal is final.

8.2 Who is Responsible to Handle Complaints and Appeals?

The Editor, Editorial Board, or Editorial Office is responsible for handling complaints and appeals.

8.2.1 Process for Handling Complaints

Initial Complaint: The complainant (author, reviewer, or reader) submits a formal complaint to the journal, usually via email or an online submission system.

Acknowledgment: The journal acknowledges receipt of the complaint and informs the complainant about the steps that will be taken to address the issue.

Investigation: The journal conducts a thorough investigation, which may involve reviewing correspondence, re-evaluating the manuscript, and consulting with editors and reviewers.

Resolution: The journal communicates the outcome of the investigation to the complainant. Possible outcomes include upholding the original decision, reversing a decision, issuing a correction, or retracting an article.

Follow-up: If the complainant is not satisfied with the resolution, they may have the option to appeal the decision.

8.2.2 Appeals Process

Grounds for Appeal: Authors typically have the right to appeal decisions if they believe there was a procedural error, bias, or an ethical breach during the review process.

Submission of Appeal: The author submits a formal appeal, providing a detailed explanation of their concerns and any supporting evidence.

Review of Appeal: The journal's editorial board or a designated appeals committee reviews the appeal. This may involve re-evaluating the manuscript and seeking input from additional reviewers or experts.

Decision: The journal communicates the final decision on the appeal to the author. This decision is usually final and binding.

Transparency: Journals may publish summaries of complaints and appeals processes and outcomes to promote transparency and trust in the editorial process.

8.2.3   What May be The Consequence of Remedy?

It depends on the type or degree of misconduct. The consequence of resolution will follow the guidelines of the Committee of Publication Ethics.

The consequences of remedying misconduct in research and publication vary depending on the severity and nature of the misconduct:

Minor or Unintentional Misconduct:

In cases where misconduct is minor or unintentional, such as improper citation practices or minor data mishandling, the consequences may involve education and training on research ethics.

Remedial actions could include issuing corrections or clarifications in publications to rectify inaccuracies or errors.

Serious Misconduct (e.g., Fabrication or Falsification):

Serious misconduct, such as data fabrication or falsification, can lead to more severe consequences. Publications found to contain fabricated data may be retracted.

Researchers involved may face disciplinary actions, such as temporary or permanent bans from publishing in certain journals or institutions.

Legal implications could arise, depending on the extent of the misconduct and its impact on funding, patents, or regulatory compliance.

Ethical Breaches (e.g., Plagiarism or Authorship Issues):

Ethical breaches like plagiarism or disputes over authorship credit may result in retractions, corrections, or formal apologies.

Institutions may implement policies to prevent recurrence, such as guidelines on authorship criteria and plagiarism detection tools.

Impact on Careers and Funding:

Researchers implicated in misconduct may experience damage to their professional reputation and career prospects.

Funding agencies or sponsors may review funding decisions or impose sanctions if misconduct impacts grant outcomes.

Restoration of Trust and Ethical Culture:

The process of remedying misconduct aims to restore trust in affected research findings and uphold ethical standards.

It reinforces a culture of integrity within the research community, emphasizing the importance of transparency, accountability, and adherence to ethical guidelines.

The consequences of remedying misconduct are tailored to the severity and context of the ethical breach. Effective remedies not only address immediate issues but also serve to strengthen ethical practices and safeguard the credibility of scientific research and publication.

8.3   Best Practices for Journals

Journals should have best practices in place for handling complaints and appeals:

Clear Policies: Journals should have clear, accessible policies and procedures for handling complaints and appeals. These should be published on the journal's website.

Timeliness: Complaints and appeals should be handled promptly to minimize delays in the publication process and address concerns swiftly.

Objectivity: Investigations should be conducted impartially, without bias or favoritism, ensuring a fair evaluation of the issues raised.

Documentation: All correspondence and decisions related to complaints and appeals should be documented to ensure accountability and provide a record for future reference.

Communication: Journals should maintain open and transparent communication with complainants throughout the process, keeping them informed of the status and outcomes of their complaints or appeals.

8.4   Importance of Complaints and Appeals

Maintaining Integrity: Addressing complaints and appeals helps maintain the integrity of the scholarly record by correcting errors and addressing ethical breaches.

Building Trust: Transparent and fair handling of complaints and appeals builds trust among authors, reviewers, and readers in the journal's editorial processes.

Continuous Improvement: Feedback from complaints and appeals can help journals identify areas for improvement in their editorial processes and policies.

Author Satisfaction: Providing a mechanism for authors to appeal decisions ensures that they have a voice in the publication process and that their concerns are taken seriously.

By implementing robust complaints and appeals procedures, scholarly journals can ensure fairness, uphold ethical standards, and maintain the trust of the academic community. These mechanisms are essential for fostering a transparent and accountable publishing environment.

In conclusion, the process of handling complaints and appeals in academic and scientific contexts plays a crucial role in upholding fairness, transparency, and accountability. In the event of suspected misconduct or procedural flaws, efficient grievance procedures guarantee that all stakeholders involved including authors, reviewers, editors, and readers have a way to express their concerns and seek redress. Institutions and journals maintain the integrity of scientific discourse and cultivate trust within the research community by encouraging transparency and responsiveness in handling complaints. In addition to defending the rights of those concerned, well-defined policies and procedures for resolving complaints and appeals enhance the general dependability and legitimacy of scholarly publications. Stressing these values promotes the quest of knowledge, fosters healthy discourse, and helps uphold ethical norms.

Chapter 9

Predatory Publishers

Predatory publishing generally refers to the systematic for-profit publication of purportedly scholarly content (in journals and articles, monographs, books, or conference proceedings) in a deceptive or fraudulent way and without any regard for quality assurance.

Here, 'for-profit' refers to profit generation per se. Whereas predatory publishers are profit-generating businesses, some may conceivably pose as non-profit entities such as academic societies or research institutions.

This is not to suggest that 'for profit' is, in itself, problematic but that these journals exist solely for profit without any commitment to publication ethics or integrity of any kind.

- Predatory publishers may cheat authors (and their funders and institutions) through charging publishing-related fees without providing the expected or industry standard services.

- Predatory publishers may also deceive academics into serving as editorial board members or peer reviewers.

In short, fake scholarly publications lack the usual features of editorial oversight and transparent policies and operating procedures that are expected from legitimate peer-reviewed publications.

It is widely recognized that the phenomenon of predatory publishing grew with the emergence of online publishing, coupled with a widespread academic climate of research evaluation linked to journal title prestige and journal-level metrics.

Although there is currently no single agreed-upon definition of predatory publishing, Jeffrey Beall, an American academic university librarian, first used the term 'predatory' in the context of publishers and journals exploiting the author-pays business model of online 'gold' open-access publishing.

Consequently, predatory publishing is sometimes confused with non-predatory open-access publishing.

The profitability of predatory publications primarily comes from a publishing fee (eg, supposedly as an article processing charge or APC, also called an article publishing charge, article publication charge, or author publication charge) that is mandatory and made a condition for publication but without the accompanying standard academic publishing services that are part of the normal vetting and production processes of scholarly publications.

Publishing fees of predatory publications are assumed to be high, but are often only about US Dollar 100, Publishing fees are typically not mentioned on a predatory publication's website.

Sometimes, instead of being payable after manuscript acceptance, publishing fees are charged by a predatory publisher at the time of manuscript submission and then banked without the delivery of any promised or standard services. Predatory publishers may even publish manuscripts without waiting for APC payments so as to build their article archive.

In some cases, there may be a misleading statement such as "no submission fee". Then, compulsory fees are announced to authors for the first time in their acceptance letter as a condition of manuscript acceptance. These owed fees supposedly pay for publishing and/or peer review administration, a mandatory set number of hard-copy reprints, or mandatory aspects of production such as copy editing. The latter may be non-existent or performed in a substandard way by the journal/publisher or by a nominated company that may have an undisclosed financial relationship with or may be owned by the journal/publisher.

Some predatory publishers also organize fake conferences and publish associated conference proceedings. These fake conferences violate all of the norms of scholarly vetting and often identify legitimate scholars as academic advisors to the conference, when in fact these individuals have no involvement or even knowledge that their names are associated with the organization of the bogus conference.

9.1   Characteristics of Predatory Publications

Attempts at definitive descriptions of predatory publishers have frequently been criticized as either being incomplete or capturing features that may legitimately exist within the complex range and diversity of scholarly publications.

Some definitions of predatory publishing say that authors are charged a submission and/or publishing fee, which some legitimate publishers also charge, but the predatory publishers misrepresent the expected level of services, such as peer review and copy editing, that are provided by legitimate publishers.

Commonly co-occurring features that may sufficiently characterize predatory publications are:

- Hidden or unclear author fees,

- The lack of quality peer review of articles by experts in the field, and

- The guarantee of acceptance and/or the promise of very fast publication times (eg, within one week or 48 hours).

- It could be argued that the main hallmark of predatory publishing is simply that there is no or minimal quality control over the scholarly material in the publications (akin to practices of 'vanity presses').

- Predatory publications are either silent about peer review or make false claims that the journal is peer reviewed.

- Another feature which is commonly noted is aggressive emailed solicitation for papers that are frequently outside of the scope of expertise of those receiving the solicitation.

- Predatory publishers may also be unethical in other ways, such as plagiarizing content in order to appear as having archived articles/issues, selling authorship, allowing authors to publish plagiarized or questionable content, and infringing or allowing authors to infringe copyright and trademarks.

- Requests by authors to withdraw their articles or chapters are generally either ignored or not acted upon (e.g., COPE Forum case 16-22).

- Predatory publishers are also known to charge a high fee for the withdrawal of a manuscript, if they withdraw the manuscript at all.

Other possible indicators of predatory publishing may include:

- Incomplete or misleading reporting of policies (including copyright and user licenses), processes, personnel, performance, and affiliations in the journal's website or correspondence,

- Poor language usage (including poor grammar) and low production quality, both in the presentation of the journal's description and guidelines, and in some of the articles that are published,

- The lack of ethics policies and need for ethics declarations, particularly related to animal and human studies, conflicts of interest, and study funding,

- The lack of any corrections/retractions of articles, and

- The lack of ability for articles to be retrieved on an electronic search platform in perpetuity, or for articles to be retrieved at all despite being listed in a table of contents.

Predatory publishers commonly advertise false or misleading information and claim copyright of the articles but only erratically publish accepted content, if at all.

Other fraudulent information may include a fictitious rejection rate, a falsely created impact factor, false claims of indexing in real indexes or true claims of being indexed in bogus indexes, or the adoption of the imprimatur logo of a membership organization with a false claim of being a member in good standing.

While organizations such as COPE work vigilantly to ensure that their logos are not replicated falsely, violations do occur. For those assessing whether a journal is legitimate or fake, initial checks should include the assessment of the scholarly status of the editor-in-chief, who may be non-existent, non-identifiable or lacking in appropriate academic credentials, relevant employment, and/or relevant experience. A further possible sign of a predatory publisher is if the owner or publisher is also the editor-in-chief. Some journals have non-professional email addresses such as gmail.com and odd organizational mailing addresses such as PO Boxes. Furthermore, false claims are frequently made about the legitimacy of editorial boards.

Problems with predatory publications range from non-existent editorial boards to fraudulent claims that some legitimate scholars sit on a board, when in fact they may have never given their permission or been invited as editorial board members. Requests by scholars to withdraw their names from editorial board lists are generally either ignored or not acted upon.

9.2   Warning Signs of Fake Journals

Warning signs based on the 16 Principles of transparency are as follows:

i. **Website:** The journal's website contains misleading or false information (eg, indexing, metrics, membership of scholarly publishing organizations), lacks an ISSN or uses one that has already been assigned to another publication, mimics another journal/publisher's site, or has no past or recent journal content.

ii. **Name of Journal:** The journal name is the same as or easily confused with that of another; scope, or association.

iii. **Peer Review Process:** Peer review and peer review process and model are not mentioned, or manuscript acceptance or a very short peer review time is guaranteed. Submitted manuscripts receive inadequate or no peer review.

iv. **Ownership and Management:** Information about the ownership and/or management is missing, unclear, misleading, or false.

v. **Governing Body:** Information on the editorial board is missing, misleading, false, or inappropriate for the journal; full names and affiliations of editorial board members are missing.

vi. **Editorial Team/Contact Information:** Full names and affiliations of the journal's editor/s and full contact information for the editorial office are missing, the editor-in-chief is also the owner/publisher, or the editor-in-chief is also the editor of many other journals, especially in unrelated fields.

vii. **Copyright and Licensing:** Policies and notices of copyright (and publishing licence and user licence) are missing or unclear.

viii. **Author Fees:** Mandatory fees for publication are not stated or not explained clearly on the journal website, submission system, or the letter of acknowledgement and/or are revealed only in the acceptance letter, as a condition of acceptance.

ix. **Process for Identification of and Dealing with Allegations of Research Misconduct:** There is no description on how cases of alleged misconduct are handled.

x. **Publication Ethics:** There are no policies on publishing ethics (eg, authorship/ contributorship, data sharing and reproducibility, intellectual property, ethical oversight, conflicts of interest, corrections/retractions).

xi. **Publishing Schedule:** The periodicity of publication is not indicated and/or the publishing schedule appears erratic from the available journal content.

xii. **Access:** The way(s) in which content is available to readers, and any associated costs, is not stated, and in some cases listed articles are not available at all.

xiii. **Archiving:** There is no electronic backup and preservation of access to journal content (despite such claims).

xiv. **Revenue Sources:** Business models, business partnerships/agreements, or revenue sources are not stated; publishing fees or waiver status are linked to editorial decision making.

xv. **Advertising:** Advertising policy is not given, or advertisements are linked to editorial decision making or are integrated with published content.

xvi. **Direct Marketing:** Direct marketing is obtrusive and gives misleading or false information.

9.3 General Advice And Approach Going Forward

Below are some suggested actions for selected stakeholders to take so as to tackle, avoid, and raise awareness of the problem of predatory journals. Authors, professional societies, and institutions:

a) Educate researchers, supervisors, librarians, and administrators in publishing literacy and about fake journals.

b) Identify trustworthy journals through the 'Think.Check.Submit.' campaign. (https://thinkchecksubmit.org/).

c) Create and continually update community and discipline-specific journal whitelists/ safe-lists using clear criteria, similar to the 'Directory of nursing journals' jointly maintained by Nurse author & editor and the International academy of nursing editors. (https://nursingeditors.com/journals-directory/).

d) Verify spam invitations, made by email, text message, or telephone call, to submit manuscripts (eg, research papers or invited reviews) or attend conferences. Consider using the DNS Checker to check the Internet Protocol of suspected spam. (https://dnschecker.org/ip-blacklist-checker.php).

e) Check journal names, ISSN codes, and URLs are real ones; verify any claimed metrics, indexed status, and organizational membership. Check that researcher profiles on institutional websites or LinkedIn mention claimed editorship of journals.

f) Read a sample of archived articles from potential target journals to check quality. Avoid citing predatory journal articles and beware when performing systematic and meta-analyses.

g) Beware of paying author fees, especially those that are suddenly demanded as a condition of acceptance, without checking what they are for, and assigning copyright to a predatory journal. Demand manuscript withdrawal if payment has not yet been made and/or copyright has not yet been assigned as a condition of acceptance (see COPE Case number 16-22. Withdrawal of accepted manuscript from predatory journal.) (https://bit.ly/2LaYOY4).

To sum up, predatory publishers pose a serious risk to the reliability and integrity of intellectual communication. These organizations take advantage of the academic publishing process for financial benefit; they frequently engage in dishonest activities such sending out unsolicited invitations to academics, without conducting thorough peer review, and collecting excessive costs without offering adequate publishing and editorial services. Predatory publications are becoming more and more common, which not only jeopardizes the legitimacy of valid research but also puts academics' careers and the public's faith in scientific discoveries at danger. To tackle this problem, scholars, organizations, funding agencies, and publishers must work together to create awareness, define standards for recognizing predatory behaviour, and advance open and moral publishing practices. By fostering a culture that values quality, integrity, and ethical conduct in academic publishing, the scholarly community can mitigate the impact of predatory publishers and uphold the standards essential for advancing knowledge and innovation worldwide.

Chapter 10

Open Access Publishing

With the goal of removing all financial and technological barriers, open access publication is a revolutionary approach to scholarly communication by making research findings publicly available to the entire world. This methodology increases the impact and visibility of research while simultaneously promoting fair access to knowledge. Open access publishing democratizes access to scientific knowledge by doing away with reader membership costs, which benefits scholars, educators, policymakers, and the general public. Additionally, it quickens the process of discovery by encouraging cross-disciplinary and cross-border collaboration and enabling the rapid dissemination of findings. Open access principles continue to drive innovation in scholarly publishing, supporting transparency, inclusivity, and the promotion of information for the sake of society, despite obstacles like maintaining quality control and sustainable funding methods. Embracing open access as a fundamental principle in academic publishing promises to shape a more accessible and impactful research landscape in the years to come.

10.1   What is Open Access?

Open access is a global initiative aimed at providing free and unrestricted online access to academic resources, such as publications and data. A publication is considered 'open access' when there are no financial, legal, or technical obstacles to accessing it, meaning anyone can read, download, copy, distribute, print, search, or use the information for educational purposes or otherwise within the bounds of legal agreements.

Open access represents a scholarly publishing model that offers research information to readers at no cost, unlike the traditional subscription-based model where access requires payment (usually through libraries).

One of the key benefits of open access is its ability to enhance the visibility and reuse of academic research results. However, it also faces criticism, particularly regarding the need to maintain high-quality standards. The principles of open access are outlined in the Berlin Declaration on Open Access to Knowledge in the Sciences and Humanities (2003), which has been endorsed by numerous international academic research organizations, including all Dutch universities and research institutions.

10.2   Open Access Publishing Methods

There are various open access publishing methods:

10.2.1   The golden route

Full Open Access Journals:

Publications are available on publisher platforms in fully open access journals, potentially involving a fee. These publication costs, known as 'article processing charges' (APCs), are covered by authors or their institutions. Most research funders support open access and may cover these costs. A list of fully open access journals can be found on the DOAJ website.

Hybrid Journals:

These are subscription journals that allow individual articles to be open access upon payment of an APC. E.g.: Bronze open access

10.2.2   The green route

The full text of academic publications is deposited in a trusted repository, a publicly accessible database managed by a research organization.

10.2.3   The diamond route

Publications are made available through diamond journals/platforms that do not charge author-facing publication fees (APCs). These journals are typically funded through library subsidies, institutions, or societies. A list of diamond journals can be found on the DOAJ website by filtering for 'Journals without APCs'.

10.3   Open Access Initiatives and Tools

cOAlition S

cOAlition S is a group of international research funders and organizations committed to providing immediate and full open access to the research publications they fund. They achieve this through Plan S, launched in 2018, which mandates that scientific publications funded by public grants must be published in open access journals or repositories starting in 2021.

Plan S allows the reuse and download of articles under a type of open license that requires no additional permissions. From July 2022, cOAlition S will support only those publishers who charge a "fair and reasonable" OA fee and provide a transparent pricing framework.

Open Access Scholarly Publishing Association (OASPA)

OASPA, established in 2008, is an international community representing OA across all scholarly disciplines. It creates and promotes solutions that support a diverse OA community, establishes publishing standards, and facilitates the exchange of information and best practices in OA publishing.

OASPA hosts annual conferences and webinars, bringing together funders, policymakers, publishers, researchers, institutions, and other key OA stakeholders.

Declaration on Research Assessment (DORA)

DORA is a global initiative that seeks to improve the way researchers and their work are evaluated. It encourages the use of advanced tools, metrics, and processes for research assessment.

Signed by over 18,000 individuals and 2,300 organizations worldwide, DORA aims to enhance the existing research assessment system through presentations, conferences, partnerships, and providing best practices for research assessment. Researchers, university staff, journal editors, funding agency staff, and others involved in scholarly research are encouraged to sign the declaration and use DORA's resources for responsible research and researcher assessment.

Initiative for Open Abstracts (I4OA)

I4OA promotes the principle of open access by providing unrestricted access to abstracts of scholarly publications, enabling collaboration between researchers, publishers, and academic institutions. It encourages the publication of abstracts in open repositories like Crossref.

Open availability of research abstracts ensures broader reach and easier discoverability of articles. Publishers like eLife, IOP Publishing, The Royal Society, and Emerald Publishing have submitted their abstracts to Crossref, supporting I4OA's goal of open science.

Initiative for Open Citations (I4OC)

I4OC advocates for open citation data, which are crucial for evaluating and crediting scientific contributions. It provides freely available, machine-readable citation data, which benefits those without subscriptions to paid citation databases.

I4OC encourages scholarly publishers to promote open citation metadata. Before I4OC, only 1 % of publishers submitted open citation metadata; since its inception, the number has risen to 88 % as of October 2021.

Directory of Open Access Repositories (OpenDOAR)

OpenDOAR is a directory of quality-assured, globally available open access repositories. It allows users to discover thousands of registered repositories by location, content type, or software used, and evaluates each repository for quality and consistency.

OpenDOAR benefits researchers by providing easy access to repositories and helps repository administrators improve their metadata and structures. Analysts gain insights into the growth of repositories and their content.

Journal Storage (JSTOR)

JSTOR is a not-for-profit digital library providing free access to thousands of journals, images, and books. Through its Access Initiative program, JSTOR offers access to institutions in 69 low-income countries for free or at a low cost. It also provides a text mining service called Data for Research (DfR), offering full-text articles, books, images, and research reports.

Portico

Portico is a leading digital preservation system that preserves access to e-books, e-journals, and other digital resources, with over 92 million journal articles, 1.6 million books, and more than 4 million digital resources preserved. Over a thousand libraries and publishers participate in this initiative.

Directory of Open Access Journals (DOAJ)

DOAJ is an independent indexing service providing unrestricted access to peer-reviewed, high-quality open access journals. It offers a list of best practices and standards for indexing journals. DOAJ benefits authors by listing journals that align with funder policies and mandates and supports publishers by providing a quality stamp. It also serves students, funders, libraries, and research managers.

Directory of Open Access Books (DOAB)

DOAB is a community-driven open infrastructure that increases the visibility of peer-reviewed, scholarly open access books. It offers free indexing and discovery services without access restrictions. DOAB is considered essential infrastructure for open science and is supported by the Global Sustainability Coalition for Open Science (SCOSS).

Open access initiatives help break down barriers to accessing scholarly research information, encouraging funders, institutions, publishers, and individuals to contribute to the OA movement by submitting their resources to open access journals and repositories, benefiting society and promoting equal access to research.

10.4   Open Access Publications

Open access includes all types of peer-reviewed publications, such as journal articles and books (monographs). Initially, the open access movement primarily focused on journal articles and the journal business model, leading to the creation of open access journals. The Directory of Open Access Journals (DOAJ) now lists over 13,500 fully open access journals. Some publishers later introduced the option to publish individual articles as open access within subscription-based journals, for a fee (e.g., Springer Open Choice). These journals offering both options are known as "hybrid" journals.

Open access for books emerged later than for journal articles. This delay is partly due to the continued demand for printed copies of books, which need to recoup their production costs. Developing a cost-covering business model for open access books has proven challenging. One pioneering project in this area was the European OAPEN (Open Access Publishing in European Networks) project. This project led to the creation of the OAPEN Foundation, an international initiative aimed at expanding open access for books. The foundation currently offers two services.

10.5 More Open Access Platforms

Major international open-access platforms include the European-based OpenAIRE, which hosts over 22 million publications, and the global OAIster, which features 50 million publications. Additionally, 70,000 Dutch doctoral theses are accessible as open-access material on the NARCIS portal, which contains 635,000 open-access publications. The international thesis platform DART-Europe E-theses Portal provides access to 800,000 theses (including those in NARCIS) from 613 universities in 28 countries. Besides open access for publications, open data is anticipated to be a crucial tool (open-publications, 2020).

10.5.1 SHERPA/RoMEO: online resource to check publisher copyright and self-archiving policies

Sherpa Romeo is an online resource that compiles and presents open access policies from publishers and journals worldwide. Each registered publisher or journal in Romeo is carefully reviewed and analyzed by a specialist team, who provide summaries of self-archiving permissions and author rights on a journal-by-journal basis where possible. This service primarily aims to support the academic research community. Since its launch over 15 years ago, publisher policies and the open access sector have evolved significantly. Open access policies can be complex and vary based on geographic location, institution, and the different routes to open access, all of which influence how and where researchers can publish their work (About Sherpa Romeo, 2020).

10.6 Most Popular Open Access Journal Finder

Elsevier Journal Finder

Elsevier Journal Finder assists in identifying suitable journals for publishing scientific articles. With a history spanning over 140 years in serving the scientific community, Elsevier's journals are widely recognized for their credibility and impact. Each journal undergoes rigorous evaluation by a Research Committee comprising internal and external experts.

JANE

The Journal/Author Name Estimator (JANE) is a freely accessible online tool for bibliographic journal selection. These tools, also referred to as journal matching or journal comparison tools, are widely used to assist authors in identifying the most suitable journals for publishing their manuscripts based on scope and relevance.

Springer Journal Suggester

The Springer Journal Suggester is a tool designed for academic researchers seeking to identify the most appropriate journal for their research. Using automated processes, it draws from a database of over 2,600 Springer publications. By inputting manuscript title, abstract, and preferences for publishing model, the web-based semantics technology refines a list of relevant journals. This personalized recommendation system searches Springer and BioMed Central to suggest the best publication match for the author's needs. The refined list of potential journals aids authors in selecting the optimal venue for submitting their final manuscript.

SAGE

SAGE Open is a reputable academic journal known for its rigorous standards in peer review. Hosted on its open access website, SAGE Open commits to delivering studies that meet the highest peer-review standards for researchers, students, and the general public. Like Elsevier, SAGE Open access journals on the site are labeled as Gold.

SpringerOpen

Introduced in 2010, SpringerOpen has established itself as a highly respected open access journal within academia. It welcomes contributions from professionals across various disciplines including science, technology, humanities, and social sciences, addressing diverse societal issues. In addition to its open access platform, SpringerOpen maintains a blog featuring interviews, insights, and analyses by researchers and editors affiliated with Springer.

To sum up, open access publication is a revolutionary step towards more transparency and accessibility in scholarly communication. Open access encourages the broad diffusion of knowledge by doing away with conventional obstacles to obtaining research articles, such as pay-walls and subscription fees. This benefits scholars, educators, policymakers, and the general public globally. This paradigm encourages cooperation, creativity, and the quickening of scientific advancement in addition to democratizing access to scientific discoveries. The landscape of academic publishing is constantly changing due to the continued dedication to open access principles, even in the face of persistent obstacles including financing sustainability and quality control. Adopting open access improves study visibility and effect while fortifying the integrity and credibility of academic inquiry, guaranteeing that research findings aid in tackling global issues and boosting societal well-being. As open access initiatives evolve, they hold the promise of further advancing knowledge sharing and driving positive change across diverse fields of study.

Chapter 11

Databases and Research Metrics

International journals serve as platforms for publishing research articles, aiming to facilitate the transfer of knowledge across generations. The number of publishers is growing rapidly, from hundreds to thousands and even hundreds of thousands. As a result, monitoring the quality of published work has become increasingly important. This task is managed by indexing agencies that maintain Journal Indexing Databases. Nowadays, journal indexing holds more significance than the publisher's content itself, prompting many agencies to take on this responsibility. However, there is still a need for more stringent filters to ensure journals with quality indexing are recognized.

11.1 Indexing Databases

A journal index, also known as a 'bibliographic index' or 'bibliographic database,' is a compilation of journals categorized by discipline, subject, region, or other relevant factors. Journal indexes allow users to search for studies and data on specific topics. They are accessible to both researchers and the general public. Journals included in these indexes have undergone a review process to ensure they meet established standards.

All databases are regularly updated, but the frequency of updates varies between systems. Each database uses its own set of indexed journals, which can result in differing scores, such as citation counts, all of which are valid and accurate. It's important not to confuse indexing databases with aggregators like EBSCO, JSTOR, or ProQuest.

Indexing databases can be classified based on several characteristics: We can differentiate between corporate services (e.g., WoS, Scopus, Crossref, Google Scholar) and non-profit platforms (e.g., SCImago, ERIH Plus, MathSciNet) that create indexes. Some databases are selective based on scientific quality (e.g., WoS, Scopus, PubMed, ERIH Plus, ERIC), while others focus on ethical standards (e.g., DOAJ, Cabell), or are all-inclusive (e.g., Crossref, Google Scholar, ResearchGate). In terms of research fields, there are general databases (e.g., WoS, Scopus, ERIH Plus, Crossref, Google Scholar) and subject-specific ones (e.g., PubMed for medical research, PsycINFO for psychology, ERIC for educational science, MathSciNet and ZblMATH for mathematics). By access type, there are subscription-based databases (e.g., WoS, Scopus, MathSciNet) and freely accessible platforms (e.g., SCImago, Google Scholar, ResearchGate, ZblMATH).

11.2 Citation Databases

Citation databases are specialized tools designed to track and index scholarly articles, offering metrics such as citation counts to assess research impact. They are crucial resources for researchers, academic institutions, and publishers. Some of the most prominent citation databases include:

Web of Science (WoS)

Founded by Eugene Garfield as a product of the Institute for Scientific Information, WoS is now owned by Clarivate. It offers various selective databases, ranging from general to subject-specific, accessible only by subscription. Journals apply directly to WoS, which determines their inclusion based on topical relevance. The most prestigious category is the Core Collection, which has four subcategories:

Emerging Sources Citation Index (ESCI) – since 2015 Science Citation Index Expanded (SCIE) – since 1964 Social Science Citation Index (SSCI) – since 1961 Arts & Humanities Citation Index (AHCI) – since 1975 Their data is published annually in the Journal Citation Reports (JCR), which is behind a paywall. The Journal Impact Factor (average citations per article) is the most respected metric for journals in SCIE and SSCI. Other metrics are published yearly, along with ranking lists within research fields.

Scopus

Scopus, a product of Elsevier, hosts a large database of academic journals from all research fields, available only to subscribers. Indexed journals are categorized by subject, and annual ranking lists are published based on several metrics, the most well-known being CiteScore.

SCImago

Operated by the Consejo Superior de Investigaciones Científicas (CSIC) and other universities in Spain, SCImago is a freely accessible, non-profit service. It uses data from Scopus, meaning the same journals are indexed. SCImago calculates several metrics, including the Scimago Journal Rank (SJR). SJR provides annual rankings within Scopus categories, and the "Q-rank" (quartile) is widely used for journal evaluation.

PubMed

PubMed is a free service provided by the National Library of Medicine, focusing exclusively on medical journals and books. It includes three databases: MedLine, PubMed Central (PMC), and Bookshelf. PubMed is known for its high selectivity regarding indexed content.

DOAJ

The Directory of Open Access Journals (DOAJ) is operated by Infrastructure Services for Open Access C.I.C. (is4oa) and is freely accessible. It includes only open access journals from various research fields, with a strict selection based on research ethics and integrity standards.

Cabells List

Cabells List is a subscription-based service created by David W. E. Cabell. It includes Journalytics and Predatory Reports, offering highly selective listings of journals.

Crossref

Managed by the non-profit Publishers International Linking Association Inc. (PILA), Crossref is an all-inclusive database, accepting data voluntarily provided by publishers. While some data is freely accessible, more detailed analysis requires a subscription.

Google Scholar

Google Scholar is a widely used free database, especially popular among undergraduate students. Run by Google, it explains its ranking system well but does not apply a selection process, which can sometimes result in irrelevant data.

11.3 How Journal Indexing Works

Journals must meet specific criteria before being accepted into an index. Although each index has its own guidelines, the basic publishing standards typically include:

ISSN (International Standard Serial Number): A unique identifier for journals that signifies they publish issues regularly.

Established Publishing Schedule: Journals must have a consistent publishing timeline.

DOIs (Digital Object Identifiers): Permanent alphanumeric codes assigned to digital articles, ensuring a stable link even if the website changes.

Copyright Policy: Outlines the rules for the protection and sharing of published work, whether under copyright or Creative Commons licensing.

Additional requirements may involve conflict of interest declarations, ethical approval statements, an editorial board listed on the journal's website, and publicly available peer review policies.

To join an index, journals must apply and undergo an audit by the indexation board. Auditors review key details, such as the presence of an editorial board, ethics statements in articles, and established processes for appeals and retractions.

11.3.1 Why Journal Indexing is Important

Publishing in an indexed journal enhances the credibility and visibility of research. Indexed journals are typically regarded as having higher scientific quality than non-indexed ones.

With the rise of open-access and online-only journals, identifying "predatory" journals has become more challenging. Indexing in reputable databases signals that a journal is trustworthy. Many academic institutions now require publication in an indexed journal for graduation, promotion, or grant eligibility.

Indexed databases are often the first stop for researchers seeking information, so publishing in a non-indexed journal may limit the reach of your work. However, exceptions exist, such as for medical case reports, which tend to have lower citation rates. Although some journals, like BMC Medical Case Reports and European Heart Journal - Case Reports, may not be indexed in major databases, they are still reputable within their fields.

Beyond these basic requirements, different indexes may have additional specific guidelines. For instance, some indexes require journals, especially those that are online-only, to demonstrate that their articles are archived (a best practice in general). Other specific requirements may include:

Publication Scope: While many indexes accept journals from a wide range of disciplines, some are subject-specific and only accept journals from particular fields.

Minimum Publication History: Some indexes, such as MEDLINE, require publishers to have a track record of at least two years of scholarly content before applying.

Publishing Professionalization: Indexes may evaluate the quality of editing and production of the published articles.

Geographic Diversity: Some indexes prefer journals with editorial boards and authors from diverse geographic locations.

Citation Levels: Certain indexes may require journals to meet a minimum citation threshold to demonstrate their scholarly impact.

11.3.2 Technical Requirements

In addition to publication standards, many scholarly search engines, aggregators, and indexes require journals to meet specific technical criteria for content ingestion.

There are three primary methods through which scholarly search engines, aggregators, and abstracting & indexing (A&I) services ingest content:

i. *Web Crawlers:* Some scholarly search engines, such as Google Scholar, use web crawlers or bots that scan websites for content. For these crawlers to locate and index journal articles, publishers must include machine-readable metadata on all article pages using HTML meta tags, and ensure their website structure complies with the search engine's standards. For example, Google Scholar only indexes articles hosted on their own pages with appropriate HTML meta tags.

ii. *Metadata/Content Deposits:* Many indexes do not rely on web crawlers, instead requiring publishers to submit article-level metadata or full-text articles directly. This can be done through forms for manual submission or, more commonly, via FTP servers or API integration, which allows the deposit of machine-readable metadata and article files. Machine-readable deposits, typically using JATS XML (Journal Article Tag Suite), are preferred for their accuracy, uniformity, and detail. JATS is a standard developed by the National Information Standards Organization (NISO) for journal metadata.

iii. *Cascading Metadata:* Some scholarly aggregators automatically retrieve content from other trusted databases, such as Crossref or the DOAJ index, streamlining the indexing process.

11.4 Research Metrics

Research metrics are quantitative measures used to evaluate the quality and impact of research outputs. These metrics apply to journals, articles, and even individual researchers. However, each metric has its own limitations and only provides part of the overall picture, so it's important not to rely on a single metric in isolation. For a long time, the Impact Factor was the sole method for evaluating journal performance. However, there are now a variety of research metrics available. This expanding "basket of metrics" includes not only the traditional Impact Factor but also Altmetrics, the h-index, and more.

There are two primary types of metrics:

i. *Bibliometrics or Citation Metrics*: These tools are used throughout the scholarly publishing industry to assess the performance of a publication, a source, or a researcher. Bibliometrics employ quantitative analysis and statistics to detect patterns in publication and citation activity within a specific field or body of literature.

ii. *Alternative Metrics or Altmetrics*: These metrics track how research outputs are engaged with online. Altmetrics provide both quantitative and qualitative data to showcase the volume and type of attention research receives on digital platforms, complementing traditional citation-based metrics.

11.5 Journal Metrics

Journal metrics, or journal rankings, are tools used to assess and compare the impact of scholarly publications. They assist researchers and scholars in evaluating and comparing various academic journals. Examples of journal metrics include:

11.5.1 Impact Factor

The Impact Factor is one of the most recognized metrics for evaluating journal performance. Originally developed in the 1960s to assist librarians with collection management, it has since become a common indicator of journal quality.

The Impact Factor is a straightforward metric that calculates the average number of citations a journal's articles receive within a two-year period. The official Impact Factor is published annually by Web of Science's Journal Citation Reports (JCR) using this formula:

The number of citations in a given year to content published in Journal X during the previous two years, divided by the total number of articles and reviews published in Journal X over those same two years.

For example, the 2017 Impact Factors (released in 2018) were calculated using the following formula: citations in 2017 to content published in Journal X during 2015 and 2016, divided by the total number of articles and reviews published in Journal X in 2015 and 2016.

How can my journal obtain an Impact Factor?

Only journals included in the Science Citation Index Expanded (SCIE) and Social Sciences Citation Index (SSCI) are awarded an official Impact Factor.

To be considered for inclusion in these Web of Science indices, journals must meet various criteria. Detailed information about the journal selection process is available on the Clarivate website https://clarivate.com/.

For many journals, the initial step toward receiving an Impact Factor is to be indexed in the Emerging Sources Citation Index (ESCI).

11.5.2   Drawbacks of Impact Factor

The Impact Factor is an arithmetic mean and doesn't adjust for the distribution of citations. This means that one highly-cited article can have a major positive effect on the Impact Factor, skewing the result for the two years. Most journals have a highly-skewed citation distribution, with a handful of highly-cited articles and many low- or zero-cited articles.

The JCR doesn't distinguish between citations made to articles, reviews, or editorials. So that the Impact Factor doesn't penalize journals that publish rarely-cited content like book reviews, editorials, or news items, these content types are not counted in the denominator of the calculation (the total number of publications within the two-year period. However, citations to this kind of content are still counted.

This creates two main problems. Firstly, the classification of content is not subjective, so content such as extended abstracts or author commentaries fall into an unpredictable gray area. Secondly, if such articles are cited, they increase the Impact Factor without any offset in the denominator of the equation.

The Impact Factor only considers the number of citations, not the nature or quality. An article may be highly cited for many reasons, both positive and negative. A high Impact Factor only shows that the research in a given journal is being cited. It doesn't indicate the context or the quality of the publication citing the research.

We can't compare Impact Factors like-for-like across different subject areas. Different subject areas have different citation patterns, which reflects in their Impact Factors. Research in subject areas with typically higher Impact Factors (cell biology or general medicine, for example) is not better or worse than research in subject areas with typically lower Impact Factors (such as mathematics or history).

The difference in Impact Factor is simply a reflection of differing citation patterns, database coverage, and dominance of journals between the disciplines. Some subjects generally have longer reference lists and publish more articles, so there's a larger pool of citations.

Impact Factors can show significant variation year-on-year, especially in smaller journals. Because Impact Factors are average values, they vary year-on-year due to random fluctuations. This change is related to the journal size (the number of articles published per year): the smaller the journal, the larger the expected fluctuation.

11.5.3   5-year Impact Factor

The 5-year Impact Factor is a variation of the traditional Impact Factor, using data from five years instead of two. For a journal to receive a 5-year Impact Factor, it must have been indexed in the Journal Citation Reports (JCR) for at least five years or from its first volume.

The 5-year Impact Factor is calculated as:

The number of citations in a given year to content published in Journal X over the previous five years, divided by the total number of articles and reviews published in Journal X during that same five-year period.

This metric is particularly useful in fields where research takes longer to be cited or has a longer shelf life. It also provides more stability for smaller journals since the calculation includes more articles and citations. However, it still faces many of the same limitations as the traditional Impact Factor.

11.5.4 Eigen Factor

The Eigenfactor was introduced in 2007 as part of the Web of Science Journal Citation Reports (JCR) and, along with the Article Influence Score, offers an alternative to the traditional Impact Factor. Unlike the simpler calculation of the Impact Factor, the Eigenfactor uses network theory in its methodology.

The Eigenfactor measures a journal's influence by assessing how often it is cited in other reputable journals over a five-year period. Citations from highly-cited journals are weighted more heavily than those from less-cited journals. To account for differences between subject areas, citations are also adjusted based on the length of the reference list from which they come.

An algorithm ranks journals based on the weighted citations they receive, and journal self-citations are excluded. Since journal size is not factored in, larger journals often have higher Eigenfactors due to the higher overall number of citations they generate. Eigenfactor scores are scaled so that the total of all Eigenfactors in the JCR equals 100, meaning individual journal scores are typically very small.

The rough calculation for the Eigenfactor is:

The weighted number of citations in a given year to content published in Journal X over the previous five years, divided by the total number of articles published in Journal X during that period.

11.5.5 Article Influence Score

The Article Influence Score measures the average impact or influence of a journal's articles within the first five years after publication. A score higher than 1.00 indicates that the journal's articles have above-average influence.

The formula for calculating the Article Influence Score is:

$$(0.01 \times Eigenfactor\,of\,Journal\,X) \div \frac{number\ of\ articles\ published\ in\ Journal\ X\ over\ five\ years}{number\ of\ articles\ published\ in\ all\ journals\ over\ five\ years}$$

These scores are normalized so that the average journal in the Journal Citation Reports (JCR) has a score of 1. Journals must be included in the JCR for at least five years, or from their first volume, to receive an Article Influence Score.

11.5.6   CiteScore

CiteScore measures the citation impact of research published in a journal and is available for journals and book series indexed in Scopus. It specifically focuses on content that is usually peer-reviewed, such as articles, reviews, conference papers, book chapters, and data papers.

The formula for CiteScore is:

> *Number of all citations recorded in Scopus in one year to content published in Journal X in the last four years, divided by the total number of items published in Journal X in the previous four years.*

11.5.7   Difference between CiteScore & Impact Factor

> CiteScore is derived from the Scopus database, not Web of Science, which leads to a higher count of citations and broader journal coverage in specific fields.

> Unlike the Impact Factor, which uses a two-year citation window, CiteScore uses a four-year period.

> CiteScore includes all subject areas, whereas the Impact Factor is limited to journals indexed in SCIE and SSCI.

However, CiteScore shares some of the same limitations as the Impact Factor, including difficulty in cross-disciplinary comparison and being based on a mean from a skewed distribution.

11.5.8   SNIP (Source Normalized Impact per Paper)

SNIP is a journal-level metric designed to adjust for subject-specific differences, facilitating comparisons between journals across various disciplines. It evaluates the actual citations a journal receives against the expected citations for its subject field using data from Scopus. Published biannually, SNIP examines a three-year period.

The SNIP calculation is: $\dfrac{\textit{Journal citation count per paper}}{\textit{Citation potential in the field}}$

By normalizing citation sources, SNIP ensures fairer cross-disciplinary comparisons. For example, citations from sources with extensive reference lists are valued less. SNIP includes citations only from specific types of content such as articles, reviews, and conference papers, excluding citations from what Scopus classifies as "non-citing sources" like trade journals and many Arts & Humanities titles.

11.5.9   SJR (Scimago Journal Rank)

SJR measures the influence of a journal by considering the quality and reputation of the sources citing it, rather than treating all citations equally. It assigns greater weight to citations from high-prestige journals.

The SJR calculation is:

$$\frac{\textit{Average number of (weighted) citations in a given year to Journal X}}{\textit{Number of articles published in Journal X in the previous three years}}$$

Like SNIP and CiteScore, SJR uses data from Scopus.

11.6 Article Level Metrics (ALMs)

Article-level metrics (ALMs) are employed to measure the impact of individual articles, including how they are discussed and shared. The ALM process utilizes a range of information sources to assess this impact.

Altmetrics: Altmetrics provide an alternative to traditional citation metrics by encompassing various indicators such as peer reviews, citations in Wikipedia and public policy documents, discussions on research blogs, media coverage, bookmarks in reference managers like Mendeley, and mentions on social networks such as Twitter. Altmetrics data is collected from the web and offers insights into research engagement across multiple platforms shortly after publication. Altmetric tracks each online mention of research and assigns weights based on factors such as the volume, sources, and authors of the mentions. For example, a mention in a major international newspaper contributes more to the score than a tweet about the research.

The Altmetric Attention Score is visually represented within a colorful donut chart. Each color in the donut corresponds to a different source of online engagement, such as traditional media, social media, blogs, online reference managers, academic forums, patents, policy documents, and the Open Syllabus Project. A high Altmetric Score is indicated by both a large number in the center of the donut and a diverse range of colors surrounding it.

Article-Level Metrics (ALMs): The PLOS article-level metric allows for measuring research impact even before citations accumulate. It assesses both academic and social engagement to reflect how a paper is received by the scientific community and the public. This metric is typically displayed alongside individual journal articles. Additionally, Scopus, a major abstract and citation database with over 21,000 journals, has integrated ALMs into its indices and collaborates with altmetrics for more comprehensive data. Similarly, Nature Publishing Group (NPG) and BioMed Central have also incorporated ALMs into their systems for evaluating article impact.

11.7 Author Level Metrics

Author-level metrics evaluate the impact an author has on their scientific field or community.

i. **h-index:**

This metric measures an individual's research output by indicating the number of articles (h) that have been cited at least (h) times. It can be used with various types of datasets beyond just research articles. The fundamental calculation for the h-index is:

The number of articles published that each have received at least the same number of citations.

For instance, if you have at least 10 papers that have each been cited 10 times or more, your h-index would be 10.

Advantages of the h-index:

Unbiased by Outliers: The primary benefit of the h-index is that it is not distorted by a few highly-cited papers or by a long tail of articles with few citations. It effectively highlights researchers whose work is consistently cited, though a few influential citations can still significantly impact the score.

Limitations of the h-index:

Inconsistency in Results: Despite a clear calculation method, the h-index can yield different results depending on the database or time period used. Generally, a larger database will result in a higher h-index, so the h-index from Google Scholar is typically higher compared to those from Web of Science, Scopus, or PubMed. Additionally, Google Scholar's uncurated nature means it may include duplicate records.

Influence of Self-Citations: While some self-citation is valid, authors may inflate their h-index by citing their own work excessively.

Incomparable Across Disciplines: The h-index can differ significantly between fields, making it difficult to compare a moderate h-index in life sciences with a high h-index in social sciences. Benchmarking is challenging because h-indices are rarely calculated consistently across large groups of researchers using the same methodology.

Not Comparable Between Researchers: The h-index of a researcher with a long publication history, including many review articles, cannot be fairly compared with that of a post-doctoral researcher or a senior researcher from a different field. Researchers who publish numerous review articles often have higher citation counts, which skews comparisons.

ii. **g-index:**

The g-index is determined by analyzing the distribution of citations for a researcher's publications. To calculate the g-index, articles are ranked in descending order of citation count. The g-index represents the highest number such that the top g articles have received at least g^2 citations.

For instance, a g-index of 10 means that the top 10 publications of the researcher have accumulated at least 100 citations in total (10^2), while a g-index of 20 means the top 20 publications have received at least 400 citations (20^2).

iii. **i10-index:**

The i10-index, introduced by Google Scholar, is a more straightforward metric compared to the H-index. While the H-index measures the total number of citations across all publications, the i10-index focuses solely on the number of publications that have each received at least 10 citations.

The i10-index is calculated as follows:

An author has an i10-index of 20 if they have at least 20 papers, each of which has been cited 10 times or more.

This metric is especially useful for evaluating the impact of recent work and identifying researchers who have produced a significant number of widely cited publications.

Advantages of the i10-Index:

- Simple and easy to calculate
- Accessible through Google Scholar, which is free and user-friendly

Disadvantages of the i10-Index:

- Available exclusively through Google Scholar

Google Scholar is a useful tool for determining an author's h-index and citation counts, while Scopus provides charts and graphs showing an author's h-index and citation numbers.

In summary, the H-index and i10-index are valuable metrics for assessing and comparing scholarly impact on Google Scholar. They offer a quantitative measure of a researcher's productivity and influence, aiding in research evaluation and academic decision-making. These metrics alone do not provide a complete picture of research impact, so it's important to consider all relevant factors to ensure fair and accurate assessments of research impact.

Chapter 12

Artificial Intelligence in Research

John McCarthy introduced the term "artificial intelligence" at a Dartmouth conference in 1956. Key research areas in AI include natural language processing, expert systems, neural networks, and robotics. These fields underpin technologies like information extraction and retrieval, machine translation, and speech recognition.

12.1　Role of AI in Research

The role of Artificial Intelligence (AI) in academic research has attracted considerable attention in recent years. This transformative technology, driven by machine learning algorithms and data analytics, is reshaping the research landscape. AI enables researchers to process vast amounts of data, derive meaningful insights, and automate repetitive tasks, thus accelerating the pace of scientific discovery and improving the quality of research outcomes.

Over the past decade, AI and machine learning have revolutionized multiple industries by streamlining and accelerating various processes through automation. In academic publishing, AI-based technologies are being developed and utilized to assist authors and publishers with challenges such as peer review, searching published content, detecting plagiarism, and identifying data fabrication. Consequently, AI can expedite scientific communication and mitigate human bias.

Moreover, AI is revolutionizing the research process itself. It aids researchers in literature review and knowledge synthesis by automatically scanning and extracting relevant information from numerous scientific papers. This not only saves time but also helps researchers stay current with the latest advancements in their field.

AI is also significantly impacting education. AI-powered technologies are being used to create intelligent tutoring systems, adaptive learning platforms, and personalized educational experiences. These technologies analyze students' learning patterns to provide customized feedback, support, and resources.

Additionally, AI has the potential to enhance human capabilities in academia by automating repetitive tasks, thus allowing researchers to concentrate on more complex cognitive activities. This includes automating data collection, analysis, and even manuscript writing. By streamlining these processes, researchers can dedicate more time to critical thinking, hypothesis generation, and exploring new research directions.

12.2   AI Applications for Research

Numerous applications of artificial intelligence have been discovered in academic study spanning multiple areas. Here are some instances of AI's application in scholarly research:

Data analysis and pattern recognition: AI algorithms can analyze large datasets to identify patterns, correlations, and trends that might not be easily detected by humans. This capability is particularly beneficial in fields like genomics, climate science, and social sciences.

Natural language processing (NLP): NLP techniques enable computers to understand and generate human language. Researchers use NLP to analyze large volumes of text, extract information, summarize documents, and detect sentiment, with applications in literature, linguistics, and social sciences.

Computer vision: AI-based computer vision systems can process and interpret visual data such as images and videos. Researchers utilize computer vision to analyze medical images, satellite imagery, and surveillance footage, applying it in biology, astronomy, and environmental sciences.

Drug discovery and development: AI accelerates drug discovery by predicting the properties and interactions of potential drug compounds. Machine learning models analyze extensive chemical and biological data to identify potential drug targets and design new molecules.

Robotics and automation: AI-powered robots and automated systems are increasingly used in academic research for tasks like lab experiments, data collection, and sample processing. These robots can operate 24/7, reducing human error and increasing research efficiency.

Recommendation systems: AI algorithms provide personalized recommendations based on user preferences and behaviors. In academia, these systems can suggest relevant research papers, conferences, or collaborations based on a researcher's interests and past work.

Simulation and modeling: AI techniques, such as machine learning and neural networks, are used to create complex models and simulations. Researchers utilize these models to study and predict phenomena in fields like physics, economics, and social sciences.

Knowledge discovery and synthesis: AI helps researchers discover and synthesize information from vast amounts of existing research papers, patents, and other academic sources. This aids in identifying research gaps, finding relevant literature, and generating new insights.

Plagiarism Check: Maintaining academic integrity is essential when submitting papers. AI tools can assist in detecting plagiarism or AI-generated content in your writing. These tools scan your work, compare it to a vast database of academic and online content, and flag potential instances of plagiarism.

Likewise, AI detectors identify patterns typical of AI-generated writing and highlight any instances of such content in your text.

12.3 Challenges and Ethical Considerations

While AI driven academic research provides significant advantages, it also presents numerous challenges and ethical considerations that must be addressed by researchers. Here are some of the key issues associated with AI in academic research:

Data Bias and Fairness: AI systems rely on training data, and if this data is biased or reflects societal prejudices, the AI models can continue to perpetuate these biases. Researchers must carefully curate and preprocess data to ensure fairness and mitigate bias in AI models.

Privacy and Data Protection: AI research often involves managing large volumes of data, including personal and sensitive information. Researchers must ensure that data collection, storage, and analysis comply with relevant privacy regulations and that informed consent is obtained from participants.

Transparency and Interpretability: Certain AI algorithms, like deep learning models, can be opaque, complicating the understanding and interpretation of their decision-making processes. In academic research, achieving transparency is crucial, necessitating the development of methodologies to elucidate the rationale behind AI-generated outcomes.

Reproducibility and Robustness: Researchers should prioritize reproducibility by meticulously documenting their AI models, algorithms, and datasets. Ensuring that AI models are robust and capable of generalizing effectively to new data is essential, mitigating risks such as overfitting and biased results.

Intellectual Property and Ownership: AI research frequently entails collaboration and utilizes pre-existing datasets and models. It is crucial to establish clear guidelines concerning intellectual property rights, data ownership, and the sharing of AI models and code among researchers.

Accountability and Liability: With the increasing autonomy of AI, issues of accountability and liability come to the forefront. Researchers must carefully contemplate the ethical ramifications of their AI systems and remain mindful of the potential risks and repercussions linked to their implementation.

Social Impact and Job Displacement: AI technologies can potentially revolutionize industries and automate specific job functions, raising concerns about their social impact. Researchers should consider the broader implications of their AI-driven research, striving for a fair transition, promoting job creation, and mitigating any adverse effects.

Dual-Use and Misuse: AI technologies developed through academic research can be applied for both beneficial and harmful purposes. Researchers must be vigilant about potential dual-use scenarios and carefully assess the ethical implications of their work to prevent misuse or unintended negative consequences.

12.4 Best AI Tools for Research

SciSpace: SciSpace is an AI platform designed for researchers, facilitating research discovery, reading, and writing. It accesses a repository of over 270 million papers and provides various AI tools. These include a literature review tool for finding relevant scientific information and an AI research assistant named SciSpace Copilot, capable of answering questions about any PDF document. Additionally, there is a Copilot Chrome browser extension that assists in comprehending academic articles on any website.

Litmaps: Litmaps is a useful discovery tool designed to aid researchers in navigating scientific literature. It creates interactive literature maps that display articles related to a specific journal article or research topic. These maps help researchers locate relevant papers, identify connections between them, and share knowledge within a particular field of study. Litmaps offers both free and paid versions of the tool.

EndNote: EndNote is a reference management tool designed to help organize bibliographies and references for essays, reports, and journal articles. It enables users to build a personal database of references and files, insert citations into Word documents, and automatically format them according to their chosen citation style.

Notion: Notion is a popular free productivity software that facilitates note-taking, organizing thoughts, and managing tasks and projects effectively. In research settings, Notion serves as a valuable tool for team collaboration, allowing team members to comment on documents, create dynamic content such as tables and graphs, and utilize its AI assistant to streamline tasks.

Pictory: Pictory utilizes AI to streamline video creation and editing, making it easier to produce high-quality videos.

Jasper: Jasper is renowned as the leading AI writing assistant, known for its exceptional features and high-quality outputs.

Murf: Murf is widely regarded as one of the most popular and impressive AI voice generators available, specializing in text-to-speech capabilities.

HitPaw Photo Enhancer: This AI-based tool enhances image quality and details effectively.

ChatGPT: ChatGPT is an AI model designed for natural language processing and generating human-like text responses.

Otter.ai: Otter.ai is a valuable tool for meetings or recording audio during work. The AI automatically transcribes spoken words and provides live captions during meetings. It integrates seamlessly with popular meeting platforms such as Zoom or Google Meet.

Lovo.ai: Lovo.ai has earned acclaim as an award-winning voice generator and text-to-speech solution.

Reply.io: Reply.io offers a comprehensive sales engagement platform that facilitates scalable creation of new opportunities while ensuring personalized interactions.

12.4.1 Pitfalls of Using AI

AI has limitations and cannot supplant human researchers. A notable example of this is generative AI creating academic references instead of referencing actual publications.

AI tools should complement academic researchers rather than replace their capacity for critical thinking. They are most valuable when researchers use them to enhance efficiency and resource management during research, rather than relying on them to write papers, theses, or grant applications.

Furthermore, AI tools can potentially diminish researchers' creativity and originality. AI operates based on input and existing research knowledge, whereas advancing science demands original, creative, and critical thinking from individuals within the field.

Moreover, directly copying AI-generated text can lead to instances of plagiarism.

12.5 Best Practices for Using AI in Research

While AI offers significant benefits to researchers, every technology has its advantages and disadvantages. AI is still considered a nascent technology by experts, and it should be approached with this understanding.

Before fully relying on AI-powered research tools, it is important to consider a few key points:

Data Quality and Bias: Before embarking on data analysis with AI, it is crucial to evaluate the quality of your input data. Providing low-quality data to a machine will not yield high-quality outputs—it simply doesn't operate that way.

AI lacks the capacity for independent thought comparable to humans; instead, it learns from the data it receives to predict outcomes. Therefore, it's essential to ensure your data is of premium quality, representative, and above all, unbiased. Biased data can skew results and lead to questionable conclusions.

Academic Ethics: Follow academic ethics diligently. Academic researchers must uphold integrity in their work, prioritizing concerns such as plagiarism, AI-assisted writing, and privacy regulations when preparing papers.

Therefore, it is advisable to verify that your research adheres to ethical standards and utilize appropriate plagiarism and AI detection tools before submission. The manner in which you write a paper reflects your professionalism and commitment to ethical conduct.

Inaccuracies: Verify for inaccuracies. Despite its impressive capabilities, AI occasionally produces outputs that raise doubts about its reliability.

At times, AI systems generate results that appear plausible but are entirely incorrect or nonsensical. There are also instances where AI may provide correct answers but fabricate their sources, termed as "hallucinations".

Such inaccuracies can significantly impact academic research. Therefore, it is essential to fact-check AI-generated outputs. Some AI assistants now include genuine citations in their responses, enhancing credibility and trustworthiness.

Human Oversight: Maintain human supervision. Despite its ability to automate and streamline numerous tasks, AI cannot substitute human judgment, context, and expertise. Given AI's occasional tendency to generate inaccurate or misleading outputs, it is prudent to have human oversight review all outputs.

12.5.1   Tips for using AI effectively for research

Researchers should utilize AI-powered tools to streamline the research process and maximize efficiency, while ensuring they do not substitute the critical thinking necessary for conducting research. Here are some tips to effectively use AI in academia:

- Verify the accuracy of content generated by AI tools instead of accepting it unquestioningly.

- Avoid relying on AI tools to compose academic articles, theses, or grant applications. Instead, use AI tools to edit or organize original content in accordance with submission guidelines.

- Avoid depending on AI tools solely to generate references; instead, utilize AI tools for managing and citing references effectively.

- Ensure to collect relevant, clean, and appropriate data for analysis using AI tools.

- Identify and select the most suitable AI tools for addressing the specific problem at hand.

- Ensure that algorithms are adequately trained, tested, and validated before implementation.

- Mitigate both conscious and unconscious human biases from machine learning algorithms prior to their utilization in research.

As AI continues to develop, it is crucial for researchers to adapt and integrate this powerful tool while being aware of its limitations and ethical considerations. By balancing AI-driven automation with human creativity, researchers can unlock new possibilities, advance scientific knowledge, and harness the transformative potential of AI in academic research.

AI has significantly transformed the academic landscape in recent years. For many, it serves as an indispensable tool, enhancing tasks like literature reviews, data analysis, and academic writing. However, others view it with caution due to concerns regarding academic integrity and potential dilution of content.

Nevertheless, AI generally aids researchers globally in improving efficiency and delivering high-quality work in less time. As language models continue to advance, AI's role in research is expected to become increasingly prominent.

Bibliography

[1] GRAF C, WAGER E, BOWMAN A, FIACK S, SCOTT-LICHTER D, ROBINSON, A. *Best Practice Guidelines on Publication Ethics: a Publisher's Perspective, Int J Clin Pract.,* 61(Suppl. 152), (2007), 1–26.

[2] *Author Responsibilities—Conflicts of Interest:,* http://www.icmje.org.

[3] SZEIDL, G.: *A Brief Overview on Conflict of Interests: https://ori.hhs.gov/plagiarism-35,*

[4] CARLSON D. E.: *Defining the Role of Authors and Contributors:* http://www.icmje.org/recommendations/browse/roles-andresponsibilities/defining-the-role-of-authors-and-contributors.html

[5] *Best Practice Guidelines on Publishing Ethics https://authorservices.wiley.com/asset/Best-Practice-Guidelines-on-Publishing-Ethics-2ed.pdf*

[6] LA FOLLETTE, MC, *The evolution of the "Scientific Misconduct" issue: an historical overview. Proc Soc Exp Biol Med.,* 2000;224:211–215.

[7] Kohlberg, L. (1984) The Psychology of Moral Development: The Nature and Validity of Moral Stages. Vol. 2. Harpercollins College Div.

[8] Rest, J. R., & Narváez, D. (Eds.). (1994). Moral development in the professions: Psychology and applied ethics. Lawrence Erlbaum Associates, Inc.

[9] Collis, J. & Hussey, R. (2014). Business research: A Practical Guide for Undergraduate & Postgraduate Students (4th ed). UK: Basingstoke: Palgrave Macmillan.

[10] Saunders, M., Lewis, P. & Thornhill, A. (2012). Research Methods for Business Students. th (6 ed.). London United Kingdom: Pearson Education Ltd., Harlow.

[11] COPE flowcharts Version 1: November 2019,*https://publicationethics.org*

[12] RESNIK, D. B., *What is ethics in research and why is it important, National Institute of Environmental Health Sciences,* 1-10, 2011.

[13] BEALL, I., *Predatory publishers are corrupting open access, Nature,* 489(7415), 179-179, 2012.

[14] *Indian National Science Academy (INSA), Ethics in Science Education, Research and Governance,* ISBN:978-81-939482-1-7, 2019.

[15] P. CHADDAH, *Ethics in competitive research: Do not get scooped, do not get plagiarized*, ISBN-978-9387480865, 2018.

[16] MACINTYRE, ALASDAI, *A short History of Ethics*, London, 1967.

[17] *National Academy of Sciences, National Academy of Engineering and Institute of Medicine, On being a Scientist: A guide to Responsible Conduct in Research*, Third Edition, National Academies Press, 2009.

[18] Bailar JC (2006) How to distort the scientific record without actuallt lying: Truth, and arts of science. Eur J Oncol 11:217-224.

[19] Fletcher RH, Black B (2007) ''Spin'' in scientific writing: Scientific mischief and legal jeopardy. Med Law 26: 511-525.

[20] About Sherpa Romeo. (2020). Retrieved fromv2 sherpa.ac.uk: https://v2 sherpa.ac.uk/romco/about.htm

[21] open-publications. (2020). Retrieved from www.openaccess.nl: https://www.open.access.nl/en/open-publications

[22] Springernature.com/gp/open-research/about/the-fundamentals-of-open-access-and-open-research

[23] Sturges, P. et al. Research data sharing: developing a stakeholder-driven model for journal policies. Journal of the Association for Information Science and Technology.

[24] https://publicationethics.org/guidance/Case

[25] Checco, A., Bracciale, L., Loreti, P. et al., AI Assisted peer review, Humanit Soc Sci Commun 8, 25 (2021).